More
Book-worm

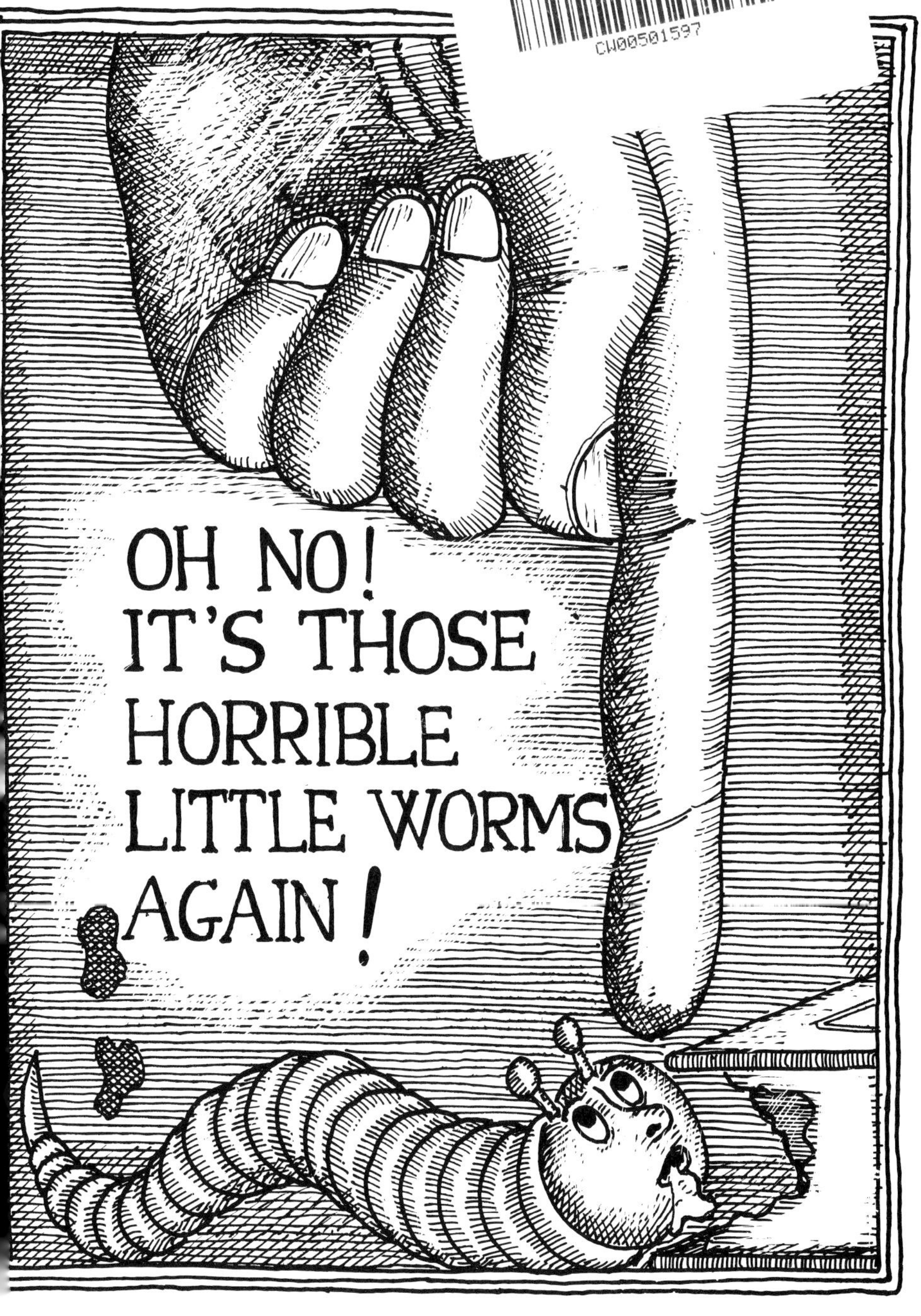

CARELESS TALK CREATES DROPPINGS

REPRODUCED COURTESY OF THE SURREAL WAR MUSEUM

MORE
BOOK-WORM DROPPINGS

Being
A Further Anthology of Absurd and Intriguing
REMARKS
Concerning Books
Overheard in such places as
BOOKSHOPS
-Both New and Second-hand-
and
in the LIBRARIES, ART GALLERIES AND MUSEUMS
of the Nation

All Offered to
THE PUBLIC
by way of a
CELEBRATION

collected by
Shaun Tyas, *esquire*

and illustrated by
THE IRREPRESSIBLE
Mr. Martin Smith

and published by
PAUL WATKINS
of Stamford.
A.D. MCMXC.
To be had of the booksellers

Text © Shaun Tyas 1990

Illustrations © Martin Smith 1990

Published by Paul Watkins,
18 Adelaide St., Stamford,
Lincolnshire, PE9 2EN.

ISBN
Hardback: 1 871615 14 3
Paperback: 1 871615 06 2

The Hardback is a limited edition of 500 copies only,
numbered and signed by the author and illustrator.
It has an extra cartoon on the endpapers.

Photoset by Paul Watkins (Publishing)
Printed and bound by Woolnough Bookbinding, Irthlingborough.

CONTENTS

ACKNOWLEDGEMENTS

The main thanks must be to all those people who greeted *Book-worm Droppings* with such enthusiasm and who offered so many more quotations, making this second volume possible. The contributors of quotations are listed opposite. Those who contributed support are listed below.

Thanks to Philip for more proof-reading and Martin for once again producing lots of cartoons. His wooden style is becoming more plastic, but the repellence is still there. He captures the humanity involved in the anecdotes. I'm still not sure whether the cartoon on page 22 is supposed to be Kinnock or Thatcher. I'm also very grateful to him for his help in editing the text.

In addition to the many friends who were listed in the first volume must be added Adrian (H.), Adrian (R.), Andrew and Helen, Anne, Carmen, Carolyn, Charlie, Daisy and Harry, David and Anne, Del., Diane, Eddie, George and Thomas, Graham, Hilary, Iain, Ian, Linda and Peter, Margaret and Ted, Markos and Sandy, Martyn, Morag, Nigel, Paul (J.), Paul (M.) and Paul the health-food-shop, Simon, Steve, Tim, Trevor. It would be silly to repeat everyone mentioned in the first volume (I hope you all agree!), but some of you have been specially important to me during the last year-and-a-half of self-employment: Anne, Barry, Bob and Pat, Dave, Ishobel, Martin, Meaburn and Peggy, Philip, and especially Paul (W.).

The larger number of anonymous quotations than before does not necessarily mean that shops were nervous of embarrassing their customers, just that they wanted to do it behind their backs!

As in the previous volume, most of the anonymous quotations were collected by myself during my eight years at Goldmark Books, in Uppingham, Rutland, and memorable incidents that happened in that shop after I left are labelled like those of any other bookshop.

There is always the possibility of a third volume, or a new edition, so please keep sending quotations! I *know* that one happens every day in every bookshop, so there's no point in pretending otherwise!

DEDICATION
For Bob and Pat Porter
friends (among many)

CONTRIBUTORS
(Including those whose Droppings have not appeared)

ALBANY BOOKS, Cardiff; DUNCAN ALLSOP'S, Warwick; ARCHWAY BOOKSHOP, Axminster; EDGAR BACKUS, Leicester; BEN BASS, Marshfield; BATTLE BOOKSHOP, Battle; SID BERGER, American Antiquarian Society, Worcester, Massachusetts; BEAUMONT-LEYS LIBRARY, Leicester; BECKENHAM BOOKSHOP, Beckenham; BELL BOOKSHOP, Henley; BIBLIOPOL, Northampton; NIGEL BIRD, Tregaron; BLITZGEIST BOOKSHOP, Birmingham; The BOOK NOOK, Fort William; BOOKS, Nottingham; BOOKS AND CHATTELS, Ludlow; BOOKS ON ITALY, Rome; The BOOK SHOP, Amersham; The BOOKSHOP, Barnoldswick; The BOOKSHOP, Belfast; The BOOKSHOP, Cambridge; The BOOK SHOP, Ruthin; BOOKWORM, South Molton; BOOTH'S, Bury; BROADWAY BOOKS, San Francisco; N. F. BROOKES, Brighton; BURNHAM BOOK SHOP, Burnham-on-the-Crouch; ALAN BRETT, London; BURWAY BOOKS, Church Stretton; BY THE WAY BOOKS, Laurenceville, USA; IAIN CAMPBELL'S, Chester; CARNFORTH BOOKSHOP, Carnforth; CASTLE BOOKSHOP, Colchester; CENTURY 2000 BOOKS, Leicester; CHAPEL COLLECTORS' CENTRE, Castor; CHAPTER ONE, Chesham; CHELSEA RARE BOOKS, London; CHEYNE LANE BOOKSHOP, Stamford; CITY BOOKS, Hove; PETER CLARKE, Rochdale; PETER CLAY, Peterborough; BRIAN COCKS, Peterborough; COTTAGE BOOKS, Cullompton; COUNTY BOOKSHOP, Oakham; DRAKE'S STAMPS, St. Austell; DUNTERLEY BOOKS, Hexham; MAVIS EGGLE, Harpenden; ENDCLIFFE BOOKSHOP, Sheffield; MARK ENGLISH, Bradford; JEAN ENGLISH, Lancaster; FACET BOOKS, Newark; T. C. FARRIES AND CO. LTD., Dumfries; JOHN FIELD, Uppingham; MARC FODEN, Stamford; FOREST BOOKS, Leicester; GALLERY BOOKS, Oswestry; GAUNTLET'S BOOKSHOP, Boston; GEERINGS, Ashford; GLANCE BACK BOOKS, Chepstow; GOLDMARK BOOKS, Uppingham; GOLDMARK GALLERY, Uppingham; GODFREY'S, York; GOODWIN'S BOOKSELLERS, Leighton Buzzard; GRAFTON COUNTRY PRINTS, Oakham; GRAPEVINE, Cambridge; GREENER AND SONS, Barry; GRINHAM GALLERY, Stamford; A. de GRUCHY, St. Helier; HATCHARD'S, London SW3; HATCHARD'S, Paisley; HIGHGATE BOOKSHOP, London; JANE HILTON, Bakewell; The HITCHIN BOOKSHOP, Hitchin; BETTY HYDE, Poole; The IBIS BOOKSHOP, Banstead; JEROBY BOOKS, Oadby; JOHN RYLANDS LIBRARY, Manchester; DAVID JOHNSTONE, Eaton Ford; ANDREW JONES, Deddington; JUST BOOKS, Uppingham; GEORGE KELSALL, Littleborough; The KING'S ENGLAND PRESS, Barnsley; KINGSWAY BOOKS, Harwich; ELIZABETH KIRBY, Stratford-on-Avon;

LAMPLIGHT BOOKSHOP, Rebersburg, Philadelphia; The LIMPSFIELD BOOKSHOP, Limpsfield; LOGOS, Sheffield; LOS OSOS BOOK EXCHANGE, Los Osos, California; KEITH MaCAUGHTRIE, Haslemere; MADE OF HONOUR ANTIQUES, Chester; W. B. McCORMACK, Lancaster; MALDON BOOKSHOP, Maldon; MARK AND MOODY, Stourbridge; MINSTER GATE BOOKSHOP, York; F. A. MOORE, Kettering; NAILSEA BOOKSHOP, Nailsea; NEWMAN-MOWBRAY BOOKSHOP, Oxford; NEXUS BOOKSHOP, Hebden Bridge; NORTON BOOKSHOP, Stockton-on-Tees; The OBSERVATORY, Sitka, Alaska; OCCULTIQUE, Northampton; PAGE ONE, Redcar; C. D. PARAMOR, Newmarket; IAIN PARKINSON, Newcastle; PAUL'S SHOP, Stamford; ROY PITCHES, Dunstable; PILGRIM BOOKS, Boston; PLYMSTOCK BOOKSHOP, Plymstock; PORTLAND BOOKS, Leamington Spa; PORTSMOUTH RECORD OFFICE, Portsmouth; POSTHORN BOOKS, Giggleswick; PRITCHARD'S, Crosby; The PUDDING BOWL, Oundle; QUINTO BOOKSHOP, Cambridge; SAM READ, Grasmere; READING MATTERS, Chudleigh; PHILIP RILEY, Uppingham; ROOM AT THE TOP, Kingsbridge; ROSS OLD BOOKS, Ross-on-Wye; A. and C. ROYALL, Uppingham; The RUTLAND BOOKSHOP, Uppingham; SALTBURN BOOKSHOP, Saltburn-on-Sea; SCARBOROUGH BOOKSHOP, Scarborough; The SCULPTURE STUDIO, Uppingham; W. HARTLEY SEED'S, Sheffield; SHEPSHED BOOKS, Shepshed; SHERRATT AND HUGHES, Cambridge; SHERRATT AND HUGHES, Peterborough; T. A. SIM, Newbury; RAYMOND SMITH'S, Eastbourne; SPCK, Leicester; G. G. SPENCER LTD., Ashford-Under-Lyme; STAMFORD LIBRARY; STAMFORD MUSEUM; The STAMFORD POSTE, Stamford; STANILAND'S, Stamford; ANDREW STEWART, Helpringham; STROMNESS BOOKS AND PRINTS, Stromness; R. STURGESS, Peterborough; THOMAS RARE BOOKS, Lanchester; TITLES, Oxford; IAN TYAS, WITH JANE, GEORGE AND THOMAS, Saltburn; UPPINGHAM BOOKSHOP, Uppingham; VICTORIA BOOKSHOP, Swindon; VOKES AND SONS, Darlington; J.W., Uppingham; WATERSTONE AND COMPANY, Norwich; M. E. WEBB, Milford; WESTGATE BOOKSHOP, Sleaford; NOEL WILKINSON, Lichfield; WINDRUSH BOOKSHOP, Bourton-on-the-Water; VIVIAN WRIGHT, Carlisle; Y.S.F. BOOKSHOP, Sheffield.

Many thanks to all of you; sorry I couldn't include every quotation! Apologies to anyone accidentally left out.

ANOTHER INTRODUCTION

"Many of the people who came to us were of the kind who would be a nuisance anywhere but have special opportunities in a bookshop." George Orwell, 'Bookshop Memories', in *Collected Essays, Journalism and Letters of George Orwell Volume I*, Penguin, pp.273-7 [p.273]

There is no excuse needed to issue a second collection of *Book-worm Droppings*, except that I kept being offered more quotes from the shops who stocked the first volume and it seemed a pity to waste them! The majority of the quotes come from the new book trade this time, with a few contributions from libraries and museums and one or two comments about books made by friends before they realised I was writing them all down. I think this second collection is even funnier than the first.

All the points made in the Introduction to the first volume still apply, but two matters require more explanation. One concerns the title and the other the philosophy of the book.

A BOOK-WORM DROPPING may be defined in two specific ways. On the one hand a book-worm dropping is a small piece of repulsive excreted waste (i.e. unpleasant useless matter which is ejected via the rear) left by a book-worm (a small consumer of books). On the other hand, a book-worm dropping is a piece of repulsive excreted waste (i.e. unpleasant useless matter but which is ejected via the mouth rather than the rear) left by a book-worm (a large consumer of books). In the former case the droppings are left inside books, in the latter in bookshops and libraries etc. In the former the droppings exist as physical objects, in the latter they exist as pieces of information or experience. In the latter case the word *droppings* also has a similarity with the word *eavesdroppings*, overheard remarks. It is quite clearly apparent that the distinctions between the two types of book-worm droppings are not particularly significant, and that, therefore the title is aptly chosen. An overheard remark within a book context is a book-worm dropping and that is the end of the matter!

Mark English has demonstrated to me that the human type of book-worm dropping has existed for a very long time, for two examples appear from the second century A.D., in *The Attic Nights of Aulus Gellius* (ed. and trans. John C. Rolfe, London [Loeb edition], 1927, vol. 1, pp.386-389, vol. 3, pp.306-311). Neither incident is quotable, but they take place when the author "happened to be with the booksellers" in Rome. And how about the following book-worm dropping from Lymington, dated 1789? The author Richard Warner has just been told by a bookseller that he has managed to flog two copies of Warner's book out of 250 in stock. Warner replies:

"Most marvellous! Couldn't have believed it, if you hadn't told me so yourself, Mr. Jones. In what a deplorable state is the world of letters! However, so it has ever been; and from the very first invention of printing, we authors, after having, as Milton says, 'scorn'd delights and lived laborious days' for the sake of 'Fame,
(That last infirmity of noble mind)
Then, the fair guerdon when we hope to find,
And think to burst out into sudden blaze,
Comes the blind fury,'
in the shape of brutish ignorance; stubborn prejudice; or false taste; quashes all our hopes; and leaves us always disappointed; and too often pennyless. Good morning, Mr. Jones."
Warner's Literary Recollections (London, 1830)
So, there you go, so long as there are books and people there will also be droppings.

The other matter requiring more detail is the philosophy of the book. It has been attacked as pompous, aloof, patronising and unkind, though perhaps not very seriously! I can only plead innocence: some humour is innevitably at someone else's expense, but if one laughs rather than succumbing to other, harder, feelings, the remaining emotion has to be one of affection.

Laughter is a very subtle thing. If you laugh at *Book-worm Droppings*, are you mocking the editor for having produced it? Or sharing a sense of joy at the absurdity of the production? In the same way, when a customer asks for a copy of *Tess of the Dormobiles*, surely your laughter is less one of scorn for the speaker, more one of joy at the idea of Tess living in a dormobile? It is difficult to say which response might apply sometimes, but I hope that the book displays a feeling of affinity rather than of separation. In the last resort it's all I could manage, but the penultimate chapter should redress the balance: it just IS the case that the dealers are very like their customers. If they weren't, we couldn't all get together to make a trade.

In the same way, the chapter called VICE, which covers quotations on sex, politics and religion, cannot be held to mock any of these subjects as such, but rather the pomposity and exclusivity which sometimes accompanies them. That plainly is laughable, but it is *human*, and if we cannot laugh at our own humanity then we are left only with mocking derision rather than joyful partnership.

Anyway, quite apart from anything else, it is 'nice to have a book in the house (I've always said it, and I'll continue to say it)', and hopefully that yellow one will do nicely!

So, another book celebrating that special combination of so many remarkable individuals who make up the book trade: authors, publishers, printers, proof-readers, editors, shop-keepers and their managers, readers, collectors, librarians, money-lenders at every stage, and friends full of enthusiasm and, here and there, wooden cartoonists like Martin. *And all of them having an opinion.*

THE BOTTOMLESS PIT

"We have a bottomless pit for these local books."
Spendthrift local librarian.

MORE GENERAL OBSERVATIONS

"Well, there's books, and there's books. But *that*'s a book!"

*I didn't think this classic could be repeated, but only a few days later
a variant version occurred:*
"Well, there's books he wants and books he doesn't. I wish he'd
make up his bloody mind!"
Impatient wife.

"Yes, Aggie was ninety when she went - she died reading one of
your books, you know!"
The Bookshop, Belfast.

"Is this library yours?"
Well, actually, it's a second-hand bookshop...
"Really? Albert! Look, there's a library here!"

Your dog, Sir, has just urinated over that pile of books!
"Oh, I'm sorry, he's always doing that in shops!"
The Pudding Bowl, Oundle.

"Oh, a library! There's a library in my home town, too, Corby, but this is quite different."
We're a bookshop, Sir.
"Are you? Well, well. Quite different, then? Mmm. What exactly is the difference?"
Well, in a library you'll find that none of the books are priced...
"Oh! I see. So, how does that work, then? What does it come down to if the book's not priced? If you open it up and there's nothing in it?"
I'm sorry, but I don't understand.
"I don't suppose you do, young man. Still, 'happy new year' to you!"
And to you, Sir.
"'bye."
[*I still don't understand what was going through his mind!*]

"What people really want to know about Wordsworth is: did he go down to the local on a Saturday night and sink seven or eight pints with the boys?"

"I don't think I've ever lit up in here before, out of respect for the books!"

"I do so love talking books, it saves so much time."
Old lady listening to Wilbur Smith through a walkman on a bus, commenting to David Johnstone, Easton Ford.

Mother to student:
"Oh! *A Question of Upbringing.* What are you buying that for? You've already been upbrought!"

...Then there was the wife who made a small purchase and said to her husband:
"Can I pop it in your bag, dear?"
Husband, not too happy, complains:
"It's getting very heavy..."
"Hell's Bells!" *explodes wife.* "It's only a bookmark!"
The Book Nook, Fort William.

"It's nice to come in here and have all your problems solved!"
[*Mmm, is there anywhere I can go?*]

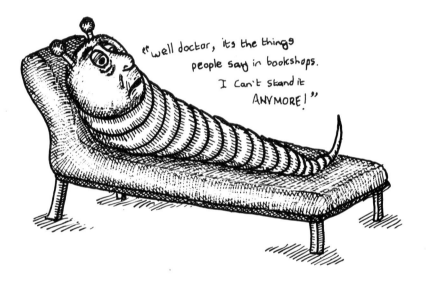

"well doctor, its the things people say in bookshops. I can't stand it ANYMORE!"

"Eee, it do smell of books!"
Yorkshire wife. Her disgruntled hubby was heard to reply from outside:
"Well, what do you expect?"
The Book Nook, Fort William.

"That's a nice picture! When was that done, then?"
About 1805.
"Really? Gosh. It must be hundreds of years old!"
Grafton Country Prints, Oakham.

A single word spoken by a man looking in the door of the shop, intoned with the same quiet amazement that one would use to say "Elephant Dung!" upon finding a mysterious pile of it in the middle of an otherwise ordinary sidewalk:
"Books!"
Los Osos Book Exchange, Los Osos, California.

"I've found some books I want; now, is there somewhere I can wash?"
The Pudding Bowl, Oundle.

"Do you sell goldfish?"
No, we're print dealers.
"Oh that's a pity. But why don't you?"
I'm not sure, but because it's the Royal Show Ground I expect it's against the rabies regulations.
Grafton Country Prints, Oakham, easily fobbing off a non-customer at a country fair.

"It's a proper bookshop this. There's books on the floor. Like Heffer's used to be."

"I don't like him any more than you do, but I want a book to read on the train!"
Overheard outside Portland Books, Leamington Spa.

"This looks like a good book, actually. You know, the sort that I wouldn't want to read but would still buy!"

"Look! Books. A bring-and-buy sale!"
Overheard outside The Book Nook, Fort William.

"This is a marvellous bookshop. Really splendid! I'm glad I don't live anywhere near here!"

17

LOTS OF VIVID DOODLES IN THERE

"This art book must be by someone who started off as a doodler. Lots of vivid doodles in there!"

"I'd rather have one book in the house that lasts for years, rather than several what don't!"
Overheard in the street, Stamford.

"You can tell these prints are old because the colour goes over the edge of the outline."
Grafton Country Prints, Oakham.

"How do you make a living out of this lot of old rubbish?"
W. B. McCormack, Lancaster.

A loud American in Oxford: *
"Ah! Gould's Kangaroos! Let's have a look at this! Oh...no... don't like that!"
German bystander:
"You don't like Gouldt? He is superb artist!"
"Oh no! Look here, we've lived in Australia and I know what kangaroos look like!"
Titles, Oxford.

"Is this the place where all the la-de-da people in Uppingham come?"

"It's like an old tombola in here!"

"Now, Betjeman. He was a real poet. People *understood* him. This new chap, well, I don't even know his name."

"I never go to the library. There's just something about library books that puts me off touching them."

"Oh! Plates! These are rather like the ones I tore out of a book in Sheffield University Library!"

"Oh! Goodness! It's a cat!"
Yes! So it is!

"I only came in to get out of the cold, but it's worse in here!"
The Bookshop, Belfast.

"Ooohhhh! I like a good read, but nothing too heavy."
The Rutland Bookshop, Uppingham.

"Yes, quite a nice man in there, for a bookdealer!"
Overheard outside Peter Clay's, Peterborough.

"You're very busy! I don't like it. Do you think you could do something about it?"

"We were just saying! Some of the books look new!"
Yes, that's right! How clever of you!

"Oh, look! 1507! It must be a facsimile."
W. B. McCormack, Lancaster.

Two ladies chattering near the counter:
"I just love all the classics, don't you?"
"Yes, my husband buys all the T.V. Themes albums to get them, you know!"
David Johnstone, Eaton Ford.

"It's like getting sticking plaster off a hairy leg, getting me out of a bookshop!"
Vivian Wright, Carlisle.

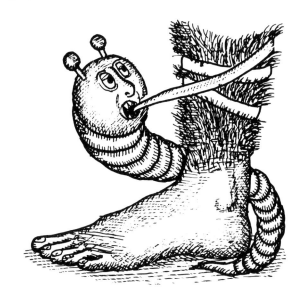

21

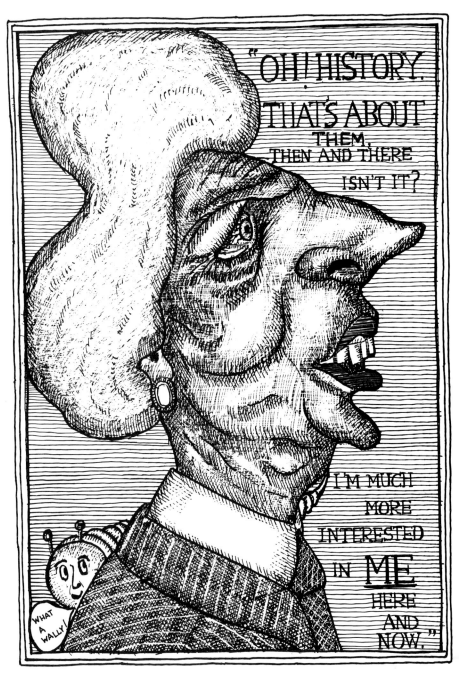

"Oh! History! That's about *them*, *then* and *there*, isn't it? I'm much more interested in me, here and now!"

KNITS IN THE BROW

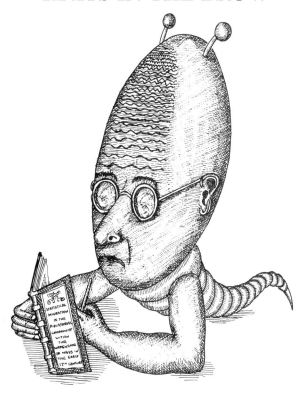

"Martin! I'm republishing Florence Harmer's *Anglo-Saxon Writs*! Good eh?"
Really? How many knits in the brow is that, then?
"At least five!"

"I just don't understand this book. What's it about? What's it mean, Dave?"
Oh, it's far too difficult to explain, but I do like Byzantine arguments.

"You know, some of these academics, they really know what they're talking about, don't they?"
Some of them, yes!

"There's a book being published, written by a friend of mine. Can you get it?"
Well, what's it called?
"I don't know."
Who's the author?
"I know her real name, but she writes under another name that I don't know."
Publisher, perhaps?
"Mmm, sorry."
What's the book about, then?
"Err, I'm not sure. I've lost touch with the author now, I'm afraid. But you will promise to keep an eye out for it, won't you?"
Yes, of course, Sir.
Occultique, Northampton.

"Ah, now, this is one of those serious books. I can tell because it's got maps and pedigrees in it. *Stig of the Dump* had maps, too!"

"Antoine de Saint-Exupéry? France's answer to Biggles, wasn't he?"

"Are you any good on authors? Who wrote *The Hunchback of Notre Dame*?"
It was Victor Hugo, I think.
"Ah yes! That rings a bell!"
Just Books, Uppingham. [Honest, it did happen!]

"Oh, gee, this George sure made a lot of silver!"
American admiring Georgian silver at A. and C. Royall, Uppingham.

"Personally, I prefer Plato to Aristotle."
Really, why's that?
"Oh, because his command of the English language is so much better than Aristotle's!"

"Oh, I *buy* books, yes, though I never get round to reading them. If I want a book to read I go to the library!"

There was an old lady browsing for a while, minding her own business, when another customer walked in and asked:
"I want a book on vegetarian diet, you know, how to lose weight if you're vegetarian..." *The old lady perked up when she heard this and suddenly shouted out:*
"Have you ever seen a small elephant?"
Burnham Book Shop, Burnham-on-Crouch

"Why have all these people in the *Risorgimento* got biscuits named after them?"
Like who?
"This chap Garibaldi and the Bourbon king of Naples!"
How about Cavour?
"Well, he was a biscuit, wasn't he?"

Irate mother, dragging her infant son away from the door:
"WHEN you can read [*smack*], then you can have some money to buy books, [*smack*] but NOT BEFORE!"
A lost sale from Keith MaCaughtrie, Haslemere.

CAN YOU TELL ME WHERE THE MINSTER IS ?

An American in York:
"Can you tell me where the minster is?"
Reported by Minster Gate Bookshop, overheard in the street.

"Have you got *War and Peace in Pictures*?"
F. A. Moore, Kettering.

"My old aunt is visiting me tomorrow. I'll bring her here. You want to listen to what she's got to say. She reads books. You might learn something!"

"So, what are you doing now, Shaun?"
I'm a publisher!
"Really? That's nice. Err.... what's one of those, then?"

"Have you got anything on frogs?"
Mmm, I don't think so, we have a natural history section upstairs. There might be some general books with a section on frogs...
"Well, to make it more difficult, I'm only interested in albino frogs."
Staniland's, Stamford.

"Excuse me for asking, but what's the best way to look after books? I've just been on holiday and I've been thinking about it all the time I was away. You see, *mine*, they get dust on the top, *here*, but there's no dust at all on the bottom! Why is that?"
Staniland's, Stamford.

The other day a customer was in and asked me if I knew how to spell a word - I picked up a Dictionary and started searching through when she asked me what I was doing - I replied that I was looking up the word -
"Oh!" [*she said*] "Is that what these books are for?"
Room at the Top, Kingsbridge.

Isn't it warm, Sir?
"Yes, too warm for this time of year. In fact, I don't think it's this time of year at all!"

"Oh! There's another book I once started to read!"

Overheard:
"I haven't seen her for ages."
"No, well she's been *bad.*"
"Oh dear, not very nice. What's been wrong?"
"It's been her *waterworks.*"
"Nasty..."
"Oh, it was worse than you think. As soon as they got her into hospital, she had to have a cafeteria fitted!"
JW, Uppingham.

The lady came bustling into the shop, clutching her handbag.
"Victorian kitchens!" *she declared, as she pulled a slip of paper from her bag.*
Just occasionally my mind goes blank, and it certainly did this time as I found myself staring at an itemised Gateway Supermarket receipt, which I then speechlessly handed back to her!
Cottage Books, Cullompton.

"You know, I think I prefer television to books. Well, it's so friendly, isn't it? Sometimes I think it's like a little welfare state all on its own!"

"What's it about, then, this *Cry the Beloved Country* by John Paton?"
"Oh, it's about abroad."
Overheard in Exeter by John Field, Uppingham.

"I want to trace my ancestors, beginning at the earliest one first!"
Portsmouth Record Office.

28

SO YOU DO SECOND-HAND CARS TOO!

An astounding anecdote about an American in Oxford:
"Look, I know you guys do second-hand books, so do you do second-hand cars too?"
Reported by an ex-employee of Thornton's.

"Have you any old engravings of Portsmouth before it was built?"
Portsmouth Record Office.

"This is an actual book, is it?"

"I know it's a long way down, Sir, but would you mind not throwing the books?"
Overheard, bellowed across the whole shop, somewhere in the North-East...

THE STUDENTS AREN'T VERY BOOKISH!

HIC

Me trying out my telephone sales again:
Can I sell you some copies of Book-worm Droppings? *Nice little book, very funny?*
"Well, we're not a particularly literary University. The students are not particularly bookish, if you get my meaning..."

Overheard from two old ladies, rummaging through the reject paperbacks in the tray outside:
"The trouble with books, *is*, you've got to know what you're looking for!"
The Rutland Bookshop, Uppingham.

"Do you know anything about this publisher?"
[*Avenal Books, New York*]
No, I'm not too hot on American publishers.
"Mmm, I just wanted to know if it was a genuine... book."
Well, it is The Complete Works of Lewis Carroll, *as titled!*
"Mmm, it will do I suppose."

"I've been and checked at the desk but they couldn't find it on the fish!"
A. De Gruchy, St. Helier.

30

"Oh! Do you sell books?"
No, Madam, actually they're slim-lined camels.
"Really? That's nice."
Room at the Top, Kingsbridge.

"Have you got Wagner's *Ring* arranged for easy recorder?"
My friend Iain Parkinson, being provocative in The Stamford Music Shop.

"I do so love books. They lend such an ambulance to my room!"
Nigel, while at Sherrat and Hughes, Peterborough.

31

"We will be arriving next week for our annual visitings. If you would like a massage, it can be left at our hotel."
Discreet message from Japanese customers of Chelsea Rare Books, London.

"I'm looking for the new book on the *Fossilised Elephant Droppings of Uganda.* Have you got it?"
I don't think so. How about a copy of Book-worm Droppings *instead?*
"Why? Are they fossilised?"

A little old lady, dressed from head to foot in brown, gingerly crossed the threshold:
"I don't know whether I've asked you this befurr, but do you sell talcum powder?"
No, we're a bookshop!
"That's what I thought!"
Cottage Books, Cullompton.

"I'll take this one. I know it's good because I've read it before. I don't like books I haven't read before."
The Book Nook, Fort William.

"Any vegetarian cookery?"
Yes, over here, Sir.
"I quite fancy this vegetarian thing, it's all chips and booze, isn't it?"

"Oh! John Buchan! He's very collectable, highly respected, too, but he's not really *fashionable* if you see what I mean..."
Modern First Editions dealer.

"I don't read, it puts me to sleep!"
Edgar Backus, Leicester.

"I *do* like Thomas Hardy's novels. They didn't call him Thomas for nothing, you know."
[*Complete incomprehension!*]

"Why should we send Fred a book? He already has a book."
Sid Berger, American Antiquarian Society, Worcester, Massachusetts.

33

SHAKESPEARE'S CAR

An American in Stratford-on-Avon:
"Excuse me, but could you direct me to the motor-car museum, please?"
Yes, of course, it's just up there, big building, you can't miss it.
"Well, that's very nice of you, thank you very much. Tell me, is Shakespeare's car in there?"
Related by Elizabeth Kirby, Stratford.

"Have you got any bus time tables?"
Mmm, not really, but perhaps I can tell you what bus you want?
"Oh no, I don't want the bus, I just want the timetables."
I see, well you can't have any!
"But I'm a collector, and I'm very well known, too!"
A Tourist Information Desk, in an East Midlands Museum...

"I'm looking for a book on *How to wood-carve a holly log*!"
Whiteman's Bookshop, Bath.

"Thank you very much for finding me the copy of the book I was
wanting, I've been looking for it for many years. Please could you
also find me two tubes of honey? The honey is only sold in jars
where I live, and also two packets of brown sugar in lumps, as I can
only buy it loose over here."
Lorraine Goodinson, Dunterley Books, Hexham.

35

An American wife:
"Has yo' got any first edition Dickens?"
Bookseller points some out and the prices. She turns to her husband who had also been browsing, and says:
"Dahlin, Dickens has gorn bananas!"
He replies:
"Honeychile, it looks as if every thin's gorn bananas!"
The Pudding Bowl, Oundle.

"Have you anything on sixteenth-century oak coffee tables?"

"Have you got a first edition *Midsummer Night's Dream*? My daughter's getting married tomorrow and I thought it would make a super present for her!"
Scarborough Bookshop, Scarborough.

"Have you got any on painting?"
Yes, a whole section, over here..
"Well, it's really the Liverpool school of art I'm looking for. You haven't got any, have you?"

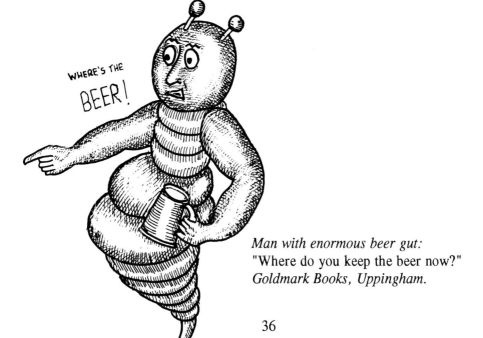

WHERE'S THE
BEER!

Man with enormous beer gut:
"Where do you keep the beer now?"
Goldmark Books, Uppingham.

36

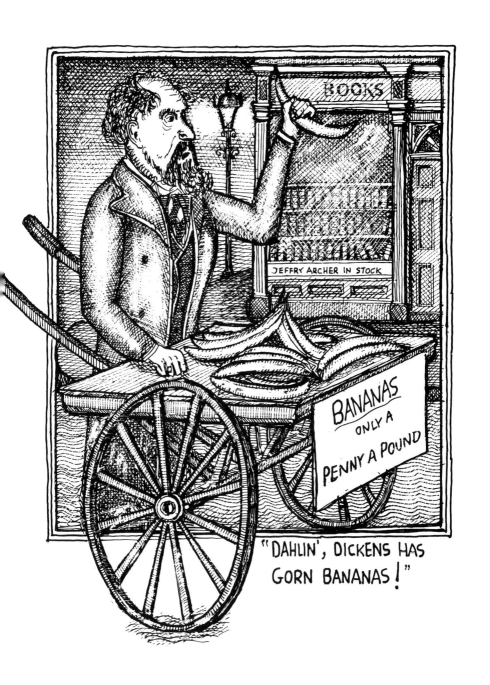

"Got any Dickens loitering with intent?"

"Have you got anything on windmills which run on sand?"
Goldmark Books, Uppingham.

"Do you have a section on culture?"

"Do you sell TV aerials?"
The Scarborough Bookshop, Scarborough.

"Do you sell fridges?"
The Book Nook, Fort William.

Skinhead with completely tattooed forehead:
"Do you buy aluminium wheels?"
Blitzgeist Bookshop, Birmingham.

"Do you have any books [*note plural*] on Florence Nightingale's Walking Stick?"
Steve Rudd, Barnsley.

"I'm looking for an A to Z of [*whisper*] *Espionage.* You know, a dictionary of [*whisper*] *spies* that will tell me all about them!"
The Bookshop, Cambridge.

Irish lass:
"Have you a jewellery cleaning service because I superglued my engagement ring to my finger and now it has a large lump of human flesh on it?"
Blitzgeist Bookshop, Birmingham.

"Have you got a French dictionary?"
[*Leaves half an hour later, having bought a Spanish dictionary and ordered a video cassette on Hindi and Bengali.*]
The Maldon Bookshop, Maldon.

Can I help you?
"Err....I'm looking for... err...some brochures..."
Yes...?
"...on, err.... holidays..."
A contribution from Marc, who works in a Travel Agency.

"Have you any of the novels by James Barlow? Normally, of course, I wouldn't read them, but he's quite a good writer. Poor man. He's dead now, of course. Normally, I read biographies."

Immaculately dressed 'County' Lady:
"Have you a section on birds?"
Over there, Madam, seven shelves floor to ceiling.
"Ah, now, without me looking, could you tell me how much they are?"
County Bookshop, Oakham.

"See thon Sherlock Holmes. Now he was a good writer!"
A Glaswegian at The Book Nook, Fort William.

"I'd like a new Chambers' Dictionary, please, and is there any chance you can find a home for this one?"
Gosh, it's been burnt. However did that happen?
"Oh, you wouldn't want to know that..."
No, really, I'm interested.
"Well, it was put in the oven."
Oh yes. May I ask why? Not that it's any of my business, of course.
"Well, you see, our oven's right next to our fridge..."
Yes...
"...and one night the fridge was making the oven rattle a lot, and it was keeping us awake."
I see...
"So we put the Dictionary in the oven to stop it rattling..."
Stands to reason...
"And a few days later we switched the oven on, but we'd forgotten about the Dictionary, and we only rescued it when we could smell it burning."

American:
"I'm looking for an early *Encyclopaedia Britannica.*"
Ah yes, Sir. I think the 1790 edition was twenty or so volumes...
"Really? Jesus! Did they know that much then?"
Titles, Oxford.

"Oh! I've never read *Winnie the Pooh!*"
"Never read *Winnie the Pooh!* No wonder you're not educationed!"
Paul's Shop, Stamford.

"Got any Boiron?"
No, I'm sorry, I don't think I have at the moment. I've got several other poets but not Byron. Sorry!
"You should read Boiron. You know 'e troid everythin' 'e did, the dirty ol' bugger!"
Overheard at a bookfair.

"I've stopped reading H. P. Lovecraft, so, have you got any Heidegger?"
N. F. Brookes, Brighton.

"I'm looking for ancient Greek and Roman army lists..."

"Where can I find teddy bears' sunglasses?"
Whiteman's Bookshop, Bath.

"I want a jigsaw puzzle of the London Underground!"
Whiteman's Bookshop, Bath.

"I'm looking for something quintessentially English to take on holiday with me..."
Well, how about Baden Powell's book on Pig Sticking? We have a nice copy of that at the moment.
"Mmm, what's it bound in?"
[*Another customer interrupted with the suggestion it was bound in a boy scout.*]

"I don't know who to ring, but can you tell me anything about waterproof hearing aids? I want some to wear underwater."

"Look, I know you're a bookshop, but do you by any chance sell resuscitation dummies for first aid classes?"
Sherratt and Hughes, Cambridge.

"I'm looking for the reprint of the Audience Survey!"
Whiteman's Bookshop, Bath.

"Can you tell me the way to the Roman bathroom?"
Whiteman's Bookshop, Bath.

Frightfully aggressive old lady brandishing walking stick:
"I want a new end for this!"
Ah, we don't stock rubbers here, Madam. You'll have to try Heffers...
Sherratt and Hughes, Cambridge. [She did!]

"Have you any postcards on hunting, shooting, fishing, that sort of thing?"
I've got a very nice decapitation from Russia...
Chapel Collectors' Centre, Castor.

Highly aggressive county lady who pushed her way to the front of the queue on a busy Saturday:
"Young man, I'm looking for books on SPITfires.."
[One was tempted to direct her to the autobiography!]

Huge man:
"Do you have a big turn over of psychology?"
Yes, we do, actually.
"I want books on AGGRESSION."

42

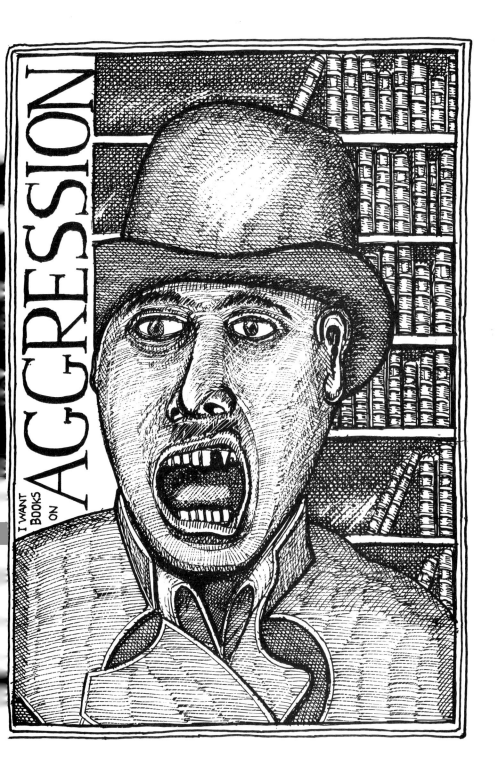

WATERSHIP DOWN

"Have you got anything on boats?"
I don't...honestly think we have at the moment, sorry!
"Yes you have! Here's one!"
Really? Perhaps I've made a mistake...
"You can't pull the wool over my eyes. I know a boat book when I see one. It's obvious from the title! *Watership Down*... it must be on boats. I'll take it!"
Gauntlet's Bookshop, Boston.

"Have you any art books? I'm looking for a book on art - one with pictures, the sort that an artist might use for reference, the sort of pictures that have been painted, you know."

How about this one, Sir? It's a mammoth piece of scholarship.
"Oh yes? And I suppose you've bound it in suede so that it's a hairy mammoth?"

"I want an inexpensive Arthur Rackham, you know, a reading copy."
M. E. Webb, Milford.

"I'd like to order a brand new copy of this out of print book..."
City Books, Hove.

"Where do you keep the books you don't stock?"
The Book Shop, Bicester.

"But why can't you sell me a bus ticket to Yugoslavia? And I also want some information on boats to Spain!"
Whiteman's Bookshop, Bath.

"You mean you don't sell Christmas tree card racks?"
Whiteman's Bookshop, Bath. [*What* is *a Christmas tree card rack?*]

"Do you sell tights?"
Greener & Sons Ltd., Booksellers, Barry.

"Do you sell hair dye here?"
Hatchard's, London SW3.

"Where do you keep the leather soap?"
Hatchard's, London SW3.

"Where's your piscatorial section, please?"

"Do you sell frozen chickens?"
City Books, Hove.

"Do you have a dictionary of Wolof?"
Beckenham Bookshop, Beckenham.

"Have you got anything on the Ogre?"
Goldmark Books, Uppingham.

"Do you sell handpresses?"
Blitzgeist Bookshop, Birmingham.

"Do you have any hat-pins?"
Blitzgeist Bookshop, Birmingham.

"Do you sell place mats?"
Sherratt and Hughes, Peterborough.

"Do you sell buckets?"
The Stamford Poste, Stamford.

46

ONLY THREE FEET TALL

I was struggling with a parcel at the rear of the shop when a male voice asked from behind the shelves:
"Are your general paperbacks in any particular order, please?"
Yessir! [without turning round] A to Z by author, top left to bottom right.
"Mmm, can you recommend a good thriller writer between K and Z?"
Yes, but why between K and Z?
"'Cos I'm only three foot fucking tall!"
Westgate Bookshop, Sleaford.

"You found me that book on the Presidents' wives, the one written in 1880."
Oh, yes, I remember.
"I was wondering if you knew whether the author had updated it to 1960?"
The Observatory, Sitka, Alaska.

"I'm looking for book-binding tape so I can mend my mac!"
Whiteman's Bookshop, Bath.

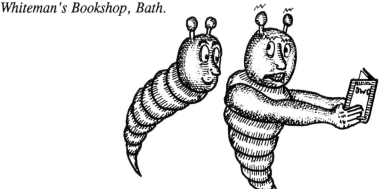

"The gentleman sitting next to me on the train had an interesting book."
Hatchard's, London SW3.

"I will give you anything you like for *Pinocchio*. Or was it *Tales of the River Bank*? Or *Wind in the...* No, *The Water Babies*? Oh dear, I'd better leave it for the time being!"

1. "Have you got Roger's *Brontosaurus*?"
Scarborough Bookshop, Scarborough.

QUIZ TIME,

OR,

THE TWILIGHT WORLD OF MISUNDERSTANDINGS

Now's your chance to play at 'shopkeepers'. None of the titles in this section are explained. See if you can identify what the customer intended... [Answers on the back pages!]

2."Have you got a copy of that book which is a bit like a dictionary, but sounds like a dinosaur?"
Waterstone's, Norwich.

3."I'm looking for a copy of *Roger's Whatsits*."
One of the Lincoln bookshops.

4."Have you got a copy of *Roger the Taurus*?"
Now old and infamous, quoted from several sources.

TESS OF THE DORMOBILES

5. "Do you have a copy of Thomas Hardy's *Tess of the Dormobiles*?" [*Now quite famous and quoted from several sources. However, for the first time in print its source is acknowledged: The Book Shop, Amersham.*]

6. "I'm looking for books written by Fighter Sexual Waste!" *One of the branches of Hatchard's.*

7. "So, what does this effing-mera mean?" *Iain Campbell's, Chester.*

8. "I'm looking for the pink book..." *Hatchard's, London SW3.*

9. "I'm looking for the works of Vilder..." *Raymond Smith, Eastbourne.*

10. "Have you got *The Rugby Hat*?" *Books, Nottingham.*

11. "Now, I want the book on the big bang, but not the one in the City..." *Hatchard's, London SW3.*

12. "I'm looking for a book (or maybe even books!) written by this chap Ibid..." *Pilgrim Books, Boston.*

13. "Have you got *The Middle Guide to Earth*?"

14. "I'm looking for a copy of *The Sunday Missile*..." *SPCK, Leicester, who have also been asked for Missile Covers.*

15. "Have you got a copy of *James Joyce is Useless*?"
Sherratt and Hughes, Cambridge.

16. "Have you got *The Book of Changes* by E. Ching?"
Highgate Bookshop, London.

17. "I want that book, err, the one with 'chlorine' in the title."
The Ibis Bookshop, Banstead.

18. "I'm looking for *Peppi's Diary* but I'm not sure who wrote it."
Bibliopol, Northampton.

19. "Have you got a copy of *Jude the Obstreculous*? It's written by Macmillan."
W. Hartley Seed, Sheffield.

20. "Have you got *that book*, you know, the one by Salmonella Rushdie?"

21. "Got any books by Patrick Leg Femur?"

22. "I'm looking for a copy of *Catch 66*..."
Stamford Library.

23. "Have you got *Learn Yourself Gynaecology*? You know, about..."
Pritchard's, Crosby.

24. "I'm looking for a copy of *The Pregnant Sailor*..."
Stamford Library.

25."Have you got the knitting book by Yasser Arafat?"
Beaumont-leys Library, Leicester.

THE YASSER ARAFAT KNITTING BOOK

26."I'm doing a sociology course and I need an urgent copy of *Marriage and the Family* by Erma Birbeck."
Cottage Books, Cullompton.

27."Have you got *Blood! Stop Bleeding!?*"
I'm sorry, what was the title?
"*Look! Blood! Stop Bleeding!*"
Mmm, I'll ask the manager... This customer wants Look! Blood! Stop Bleeding! *Do you know it?*
Ah yes! I know the one you want, Sir, over here...
A nice misinterpretation by the staff at Battle Bookshop, Battle.

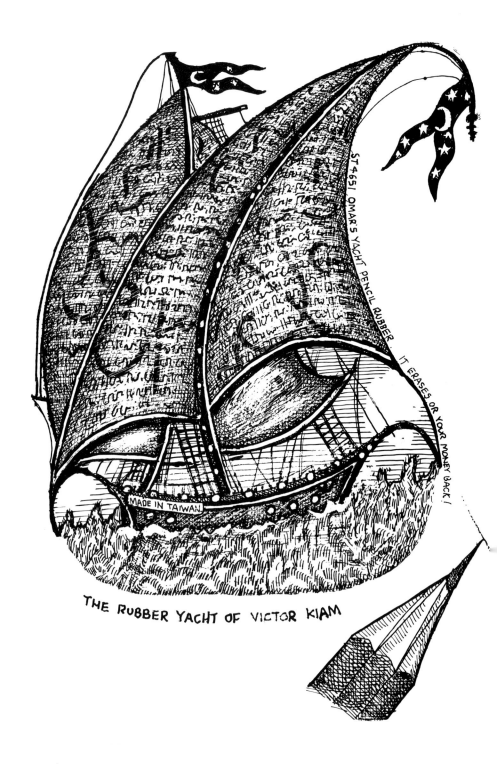

THE RUBBER YACHT OF VICTOR KIAM

28. "My son would like to know if you've got a copy of *The Rubber Yacht of Victor Kiam.*"
Westgate Bookshop, Sleaford.

29. "I'm looking for a book about London, and it's got a picture on the front cover with the Guards and The Beatles on (together), and I saw it in the show case at the Berkeley Hotel eighteen months ago."
Hatchard's, London SW3.

30. "Have you got *The Whirley-Washers*?"
Scarborough Bookshop, Scarborough.

31. "It's a true story about a man."
Hatchard's, London SW3.

32. "Got any of them books by George Mee?"
Staniland's, Stamford.

33. "Have you got Theodore Sturgeon's *Not Without Surgery*?"
David Johnstone, Eaton Ford.

34. "I have a rare book of 1152!"
Really? Gosh! What sort of a book is it? Theology?
"No, it's about ghosts, I think."
Wow! In Latin?
"No, English."
English? How ... unusual. Is it a manuscript, then?
"No, printed, of course. You know, it's a *book*."
Err, are you sure of the date?
"Yes, of course, it says so on it. 1152!"
Really? In Roman numerals I suppose?
"No, ordinary numbers. I know it's old because the photograph on the back is faded!"
Vokes and Sons, Darlington. Can you identify the book?

35. "I don't know what it's called and I don't know who wrote it, but the girl on television had long dark hair."
The Book Shop, Ruthin.

36. "I'm looking for a copy of *To a Garden Gnome* by [*famous American novelist*]."
Steve Rudd, Barnsley.

37. "I'm looking for books by Sir Arthur Coal-and-oil."

38. "Have you got *Up Dee's Backie*?"
Sherratt and Hughes, Cambridge.

39. "I'm looking for *Shunnokkassie*..."
Sherratt and Hughes, Cambridge.

40. "Have you got *The Captain of the Brass Band's Conversation*?"
Marjorie Anderson, St. Andrew's.

41. "Where do you keep *Howard's Way*?"
Cambridge again.

42. "I can't remember the author, but I know the surname began with a letter between K and R."
Jeroby Books, Oadby.

43. "Have you got any of the books by Amos Kingsley?"
Gauntlet's Bookshop, Boston.

44. "I want a history of the world by ..., err, by someone whose name ends in S!"
Goldmark Books, Uppingham.

45. "Have you got any of the Narnia novels by C. S. Lewis? My daughter wants one."
Yes, I think we've got them all. Which one did you want?
"I want *Lionel Richie and the Wardrobe...*"
Reported by T. C. Farries and Co., Ltd., Dumfries

46. "Have you got *The Book of Revolutions*? It's a religious book."
Stamford Library.

47. "Got any books by Itchiebits?"
Iain Campbell, Chester. You can work it out.

48. *Overheard in a Suffolk bookshop, between proprietor and visiting bookseller:*
"Do you by any chance have a "Book of the Film"-type of title on *I Could Go on Singing*, you know, the last film Judith Garfield made when she starred with Derek Beauregarde?"
Quoted by C. D. Paramor, Newmarket.

49. "Have you got a copy of *Donkey's Oats*?"
Staniland's, Stamford.

A BIBLE
WITH
APOTHECARY

50. "Can I have a *New English Bible*, the one with the Apothecary, please?"
Goodwin's Booksellers, Leighton Buzzard.

51. "Where do you keep the books by Evelyn Waff? Doesn't she write well?"
Staniland's, Stamford, and a similar quote from The Bell Bookshop, Henley.

52. "I'm looking for that German writer, Go-eath..."
Staniland's, Stamford.

53. "Got anything on hoggaboggammy wardrobes?"
JW, Uppingham.

54. "Anything by the Irish Murdoch?"
Ben Bass, Marshfield.

55. "Have you got the book about Mulligan? The explorer?"
Stamford Library.

56. "Got any new books by John le Carrier?"
Plymstock Bookshop, Plymstock.

57. "Do you have any books by Nostromo?"
Sherratt and Hughes, Cambridge.

58. "Have you got anything by Green Hathaway?"
M. E. Webb, Milford.

59. "Mummy! Who was Oscar Wilde?"
"He was the chap who wrote *The Owl and the Pussy Cat* and lots of other things like it, dear!"
Overheard at Reading Matters, Chudleigh.

60. "I don't know the author or the title but in it a man was kicked by a giraffe!"
Sam Read, Grasmere.

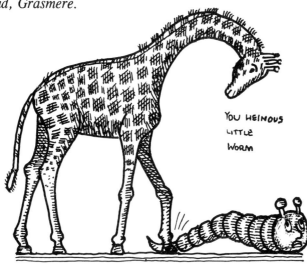

61. "Could I have the latest Frederick Forsyth?"
You mean The Fourth...
"I don't know the title, but it is something to do with a tiger, you know the chap who writes about Africa."
Ah, you mean ...
Roy Pitches, Dunstable.

62. "I'll have that *Dictionary of Brewing* in the window, the one that considers the Phrase and Fable of Brewing."
Endcliffe Bookshop, Sheffield.

63. "I'm looking for a copy of *Love in a Cholera Climate...*"
Hatchard's, London SW3.

64. "Isn't Marc Chagall a perfume?"

65. "Do you have (and if not, can you get me a copy?) of that funny book of bedtime stories?"
Room at the Top, Kingsbridge.

66. *An overseas visitor in Oxford:*
"You have *Not a book*?"
We have lots of books, Sir!
"Not a book?"
We have, err, posters.
"You have Not a Book?"
This is *the title of a book, Sir? No I'm afraid not.*
"But I see them! I see them there! Yes?"
Ahh, right. Thank you, that's £1.20 please.
Newman-Mowbray Bookshop, Oxford.

67. "Have you got a copy of *The Lemon Curd of Karanda*?"
The Hitchin Bookshop, Hitchin.

OUT AND ABOUT WITH THE GUIDE TO SMALL SQUASHED THINGS YOU FIND ON MOTORWAYS

68."Have you got *The Collins' Field Guide to Small Squashed Things You Find on Motorways?*"
Hatchard's, London SW3.

69."Can you help me, please? I want *J. M. Barrie and the Lost Bags*"
Hatchard's, London SW3.

70."Have you got a copy of *Krenger's Elk?*"
Hatchard's, London SW3.

HARASSING THE PEACOCK

71. *The widow of [famous author] asked in a Tokyo bookstore several years ago if they had any of her late husband's books. 'Indeed we do', came the reply, 'his most famous book we have:* The Angry Raisins.'
Reported by T. A. Sim, Newbury.

72."I'm searching for a copy of *Harassing the Peacock.*"
Oh, don't you mean Raising the Peacock, *Sir?*
"No, I'm sure it was harassing…"
Hatchard's, London SW3.

73."Now, have you got *Julia Margaret Cameron: Her Lice and Photographic Work?*"
Hatchard's, London SW3.

74."I want the book with the red helmet and the handcuffs on it, which I was told about in the pub five years ago!"
Nailsea Bookshop, Nailsea.

75."I'm looking for *Young Men in Spots.*"
Hatchard's, London SW3.

76."Have you got a copy of *The Man who ate his Wife's Hat?*"
Hatchard's, London SW3.

77."I can't remember the author's name - and they're all by different ones, aren't they?"
Gallery Books, Oswestry.

OH CRUMBS! ITS THE ANGRY RAISINS! AND THEY'RE JOLLY ANGRY!

EDWARD GETS THE BOOKS DOWN FROM THE TOP SHELF

MONEY

*MORE BUYING AND SELLING
AND HAGGLING OVER PRICE*

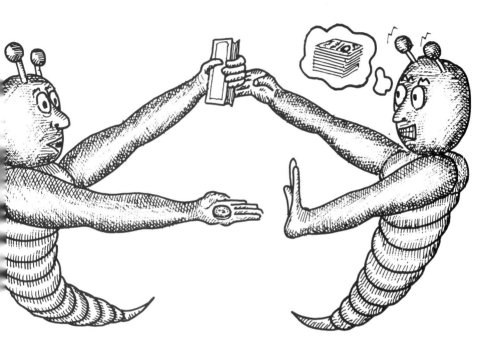

*Three schoolboys, one tall, one small and the other medium height.
They browsed for about half an hour, then the tall one went out. The
small one got very upset and ran off after him shouting:*
"Edward! Stop! I haven't finished yet! There's another room I
haven't been in. Edward! Where are going? Oh, come on!
Edward!"
*And they disappeared out of the door. Then the medium-sized one
who was left came up to me and discreetly whispered:*
"You see, Edward is the one who gets the books down from the top
shelf for him!"

"Would you accept half of what you're asking, because I think I
may have read it?"
Peter Clarke, Rochdale.

I have a small customer who occasionally pops into the shop when walking home from work (he lives a further mile away). He refuses to pay any more than 10p for a book and even then begrudgingly. On this particular day he spotted a stack of about forty tatty National Geographics *which I had piled up ready to take to the tip the next day...*
"I bet they're expensive!"
20 pence each, but 50% discount if you buy the lot!
"Mmm..."
100% discount if you buy them and take them away now. That is, free, to a customer such as yourself!
"Free? Then I can't say no!"
O.K., now hold out your arms, there! Pity I've no boxes at the moment. Good day!
Westgate Bookshop, Sleaford.

Vendor trying his best to get a good price:
"These are very old friends and I'm not going to part with them easily!"
Goldmark Books, Uppingham.

Another determined seller of second-hand books:
"These are my wife's. She doesn't want me to have any money so we have to keep them separate."
Goldmark Books, Uppingham.

Yet another hopeful vendor:
"Look at this one: COMPLETELY UNOBTAINABLE!"
I'm sorry, Sir, but we seem to have another completely unobtainable on the shelf at the moment.
Goldmark Books, Uppingham.

First-time customer upon handing over a book titled Do your own Bankruptcy:
"Will you take a cheque?"
Los Osos Book Exchange, Los Osos, California

Scruffy man, bearing box of books:
"I was just on my way to the tip with these 'ere books, when I saw your shop. I thought you'd like to buy them."
How kind! Mmm. They're a bit rough, but I'll offer you two pounds.
"Two quid! I might as well throw them away for that!"
[*And he did!*] *Westgate Bookshop, Sleaford.*

A customer clutching a plastic carrier bag:
"Do you sell bric-a-bracs?"
Yes, Sir.
"So, do you buy bric-a-bracs?"
Yes, Sir.
"Oh good, 'cos I've got one!"
The Pudding Bowl, Oundle.

"Mum! What 'xactly do we sell here?"
Well, mainly old books...
"Oh. Well, if you sell old books, can I sell young books?"
Room at the Top, Kingsbridge.

Customer absolutely thrilled to bits to find a copy of Dixon's History of Freemasonry in Lincolnshire, *at £27.50:*
"Oh! Tremendous! I've been looking for this for years. Anything you can do on the price?"
No.
"Thought you wouldn't - there's a copy round the corner for £60!"
At the Stamford Book Fair.

An old and well-known customer once came to sell me a handful of books for which I offered £15...
"Is that an offer or an opening bid?" *was his reply, made in all innocence. I assured him that it was a firm offer.* "Oh!" [*He said*] "I thought I was expected to bargain like they do in the East."
Castle Bookshop, Colchester.
[*Note from the editor: In some shops you are!*]

Can I help you?
"No, it's all right. I'm just thinking. Bookshops are good places for thinking."

"Does your bookshop buy wartime cigarette cards stuck in their original books? I realise I open myself to ridicule in asking this..."

"How much is this book? I got it from the box out the front of the shop."
That's just ten pence, please.
"Ten pence? That's cheap! Take twenty pence instead; after all, you've a living to make!"
Westgate Bookshop, Sleaford.

"I'm ringing to inquire about a book I want. I'm afraid we've lost our old copy."
Oh dear, what happened?
"Well, I had a copy until yesterday when the wife put it in the washing machine!"
But why? Was it a very small book?
"Not at all, it was a hardback of about 250 pages, and about 10" by 6". She'd changed the bed covers and, as I'd been reading it in bed, in went the book as well!"
Amazing customer of Nigel Bird, Tregaron.

Opening time, Wednesday morning, an elderly gentleman dumps a folded wheelchair in front of the counter and complains:
"It wouldn't work! We 'ad to borrow one from Flamingo Park Zoo!"
Saltburn Bookshop, Saltburn.

"Do you buy books here?"
Yes we do!
"Oh good. Would you like these copies of *The War Cry*?"

"I'LL HAVE THAT BOOK AFTERALL"

Husband to wife: "Would you shoot me if I bought this?"
Wife: "Well, I think you should think very carefully indeed about that. Very carefully. You've got two lovely books at home. I don't see any reason at all why you should want a third. And where would we put it?"
"Oh, all right, then, I'll think about it..."
Three days later he rang to say he'd been thinking about it and had decided to buy it, and would we put it aside for him. Quite right, too.

70

It was a grim winter's evening and I was about to close when a retired-army-colonel-type threw open my door and started lobbing in box after box of quite good quality books...
"My wife insists I get rid of these, they've been in the garage for ages, so you can have them!"
Well, if you hang on a minute I'll make you an offer...
"No time for that! Have them for free. Anyway, the dog's probably pissed on them. Good night!"
Westgate Bookshop, Sleaford.

"I went past your shop the other day, and I really admired the books in the window... and I was wondering; what do you charge for a week's rental on any book?"
Staniland's, Stamford.

"I feel myself just *itching* to write you a really big cheque, so I'm going home!"
[Goes away but returns later same day and buys desired book for £12]
"I feel so naughty!"

"Would you take 75p for this post card? After all, you're not going to sell it!"
Chapel Collectors' Centre, Castor.

"Do you sell maps?"
Yes, Madam.
"Well, where are they, then?"
Right next to you!
"Oh yes; but you haven't got the one I want!"
Oh dear, which was that?
"I want the street plan for Sydney."
Archway Bookshop, Axminster.

"It says £10 on this one. What will you take for it?"
Vivian Wright, Carlisle.

"Can you knock anything off this? It's marked at ninety pee?"
Really? How much had you in mind?
"Seven pence."
Oh, all right then, eighty-three pence!
"No, I've only got seven pence!"
Westgate Bookshop, Sleaford.

Pompous, middle-aged man in pin-striped suit after half-an-hour's browsing:
"I'll give you five pounds for these two books, and that's more than they're worth!"
Then you won't want to waste your money! Good Bye!
Westgate Bookshop, Sleaford.

Customer with strong Scots accent:
"Ah'm leukin f'r buiks of Reurrbins..."
[*Bookseller shows Reubens, the artist*]
"Nah, Aye didne want that. I wannered Harold Reurrbins, but ahl take it anyway!"
Stromness Books and Prints, Stromness [Harold Robbins].

"Excuse me, I've just come out of hospital. I've got a false arm and a false leg, and can you give me £12?"
Hatchard's, Paisley.

RAF man:
"I've got some gash books for sale..."
Ah, how many?
"Oh, ten, twelve, maybe fourteen."
Well, why not bring them round in a bag and I'll have a look at them?
"Err, no, I meant fourteen tons."
Westgate Bookshop, Sleaford.

"Do you sell reading books?"
Edgar Backus, Leicester.

"I suppose this is a hobby. Do you have a pension?"
Vivian Wright, Carlisle.

Man with a large cast on his leg, hobbling into the shop and carrying a large box:
"Do you want to buy some karate books, cheap?"
Los Osos Book Exchange, Los Osos, California

"Could I please use your toilet? I'm pissing myself at the prices in those Hentys!"
The Pudding Bowl, Oundle.

"We've got so many books at home we've no room for any more! We've got one shelf on the landing and another under the stairs!"
Vivian Wright, Carlisle.

I'm sorry, but I cannot buy these books because I have reason to believe they belong to the School Library!
"Oh! I know! But it's so tedious taking them back, isn't it?"
Goldmark Books, Uppingham.

Thank you, that's £2.75, please.
"Oh! I've only got £2.50, will that do?"
All right, then.
"Look, I've got nine pence here, you couldn't swap it me for a ten pence piece, could you?"
I think that would be adding insult to injury.

Gentleman with a surgical collar visits the shop on three consecutive days, leisurely browsing one hour at a time, but not buying:
"I bet you wonder why I come here."
Why do you?
"I find that looking at books exercises my neck."
Feel free to try the light flex!
Blitzgeist Bookshop, Birmingham.

"Fifty pence! I can't afford that! I only earn £6 an hour on my policeman's wage, and everytime I go out of the house I RISK MY LIFE!"
One of Ernie's customers, Saltburn-by-the-Sea.

A Socratic dialogue from Los Osos Book Exchange, Los Osos, California:

[Enter. Casually-Dressed-Young-Man-With-Conspiratorial-Air, closing the open door behind him despite the spring warmth. Glances down the first aisles and toward the back of the shop:] "Hi."

[Startled-Book-Shop-Owner-Who-Had-Been-Reading,-Feet-on-Desk,-Peaches-the-Cat-on-Lap. Currently reading a review of a new book on Nostratic language theories:] Hello.

CDYMWCA: "You the owner?"

SBSO,WHBR,FOD,PTCOL: Yes. Buy and take trade-ins. Always. Can't sell from an empty wagon.

CDYMWCA: *[Not at all amused]* "I got these for sale." *[Pulls four very small hardcover books from his jacket pocket. Red cloth covers, black lettering and "flowering". Hands them to SBSO,WHBR,FOD,PTCOL.]*

SBSO,WHBR,FOD,PTCOL: [Instantly recognises the type, if not these exact books. Miscellaneous survivors from an early-twentieth-century set of "great culture and great ideas", designed to give a feeling of culture and comfort to the aspiring lower and middle classes of that innocent time before world wars and world depressions and AIDS. Usually printed with "loud" covers and cheap materials. Looked great on the shelf for about a week, but then they started to get dusty. Moved to the attic about 1932, *one-half of one-book read. Now almost literally a dime a dozen. Vol. III: Emerson's Essays; Vol. VI: Thoreau on Nature; Vol. XI, Scenes from Dickens; Vol. XXII, The Roman Laws. Total value and total possibility of selling them, zero. Still, SBSO,WHBR,FOD,PTC-OL, hating to turn anyone away, figures he can give $1 for the four and still not deprive his family of food:]* Humm...

CDYMWCA: [Leaning forward, speaking quietly:] "They're real rare, a buddy told me. You can have them for $5,000. Each."

SBSO,WHBR,FOD,PTCOL: Humm....

CDYMWCA: [Quickly, perhaps recognising the stunned tone in the "Humm"] "But I'm in kinda a hurry to sell them. They're from my grandmother's estate. You can have them for $6,000 for all. They're worth it. Really, a buddy told me."

SBSO,WHBR,FOD,PTCOL: [Realising that something is very wrong indeed, and hoping that he can get out of this physically unharmed:] Ah. Ah. Ah: maybe so, but I don't think I can give that for them. This is a pretty small shop.

CDYMWCA: "Yeah. I know. You gotta make a buck too. How about $100 for the four?"

SBSO,WHBR,FOD,PTCOL: I'm afraid I can't even go that. They were pretty widely published and distribu...

CDYMWCA: "Listen, my folks can help me out till I get back on my feet. Gimme $25 and they're yours."

SBSO,WHBR,FOD,PTCOL: I just don't think I can use them here. Sorry.

CDYMWCA: [Opening door, glancing out, and starting to leave. Words over his shoulder:] "Well, one thing I know, I'm sure glad they're not stolen."

Los Osos Book Exchange, Los Osos, California.

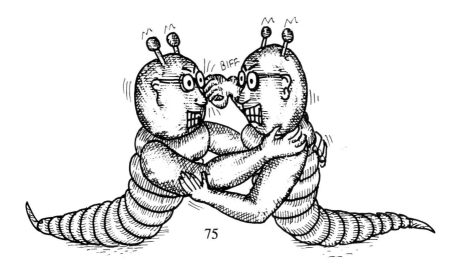

Customer, having spent nearly two hours gathering together a pile of some thirty or forty books, came up and placed them all on the counter and announced:
"I don't want these. Thank you."
Occultique, Northampton.

SOFT BACKS
SPINELESS EXCUSES FOR NOT BUYING

"Hello, I'm ringing to ask if you have any Greek lexicons?"
Yes, we have a small one at £3.50 and a great big one at £10...
"Oh. Mmm. When you say 'great big one' do you mean 'really huge' as in, err, 'great big hardbacks'?"
Yes, that's right!
"Great, well thanks a lot. Goodbye." [*click*]

Wife:
"See anything you want, dear?"
Husband:
"There's one here for Charlie, but it's £4 and he's not worth that!"
The Book Nook, Fort William.

"Thank you, but I will not listen to Bach while looking at books!"
Irritable non-buyer, while walking out.

"Do you have the novel by Abu Abeke?"
No, but I could order it for you.
"Actually, I'm hoping to borrow it."
Bookworm, South Molton.

"Have you got *Seven Pillars of Wisdom*?"
Yes! I think we have. Here it is!
"Oh no! I didn't realise it was as big as that. No, we've got too many big books in the house already..."

"We were waiting outside for you. We just couldn't stand the smell!"
Overheard whisper as a customer was reunited with his family at the front door!

"I don't care for books. They're harbingers of dust."

"Hey! This is a good book. I'll buy it in Burnley!"
The Bookshop, Barnoldswick.

"I wouldn't have this book if it was in a Lucky Bag!"

"I don't suppose you've got any astronomy for me?"
Yes! This time, we have!
"Oh... err, how much is that then?"
Ten pence! What I paid for it!
"Mmm, it's a bit grubby..."
Westgate Bookshop, Sleaford.

"You can't sell that, it's dirty! Look, it's got blood on it!"
Oh? So it has, it must be one of those 'Scratch and Sniff' ones!
Cheyne Lane Bookshop, Stamford.

"Have you got a copy of *Hilda Lessways* by Arnold Bennett?"
Hang on a moment, please...Oh yes, we do, here it is and only
£3.50.
"But I only wanted it to read! Tell you what, I'll read it and bring it
straight back, how's that?"
What?
"Oh, well, I'll try that other shop round the corner and see if they
have one, cheaper, but I might come back to you."

"I like really well-used library books because they always fall flat,
staying open at the right page; by far the easiest thing to read. This
one's dreadful. I'd have to use me mug of tea to keep it down.
Most uncomfortable!"
Overheard at Duncan Allsop's, Warwick.

"Can you keep it on order and I'll try and get it elsewhere!"
Mark and Moody, Stourbridge.

"I haven't read it all, but I've played around with it, so I think I'd better leave it!"

"Have you got a copy of *Life on an African Farm*?"
Yes, in Penguin, over here...
"No, I wanted the Virago edition. I've only got five minutes and I wanted to read the Introduction."
City Lit Bookshop, London.

"Have you got anything on Eastern Brass Ware?"
Yes! We have! Here you are, The Brass Industry in Uttar Pradesh.
"Oh, come off it, I've only got two pee!"

"Do you think the Library will have this one?"
Occultique, Northampton.

"It's a super book, and I'd *love* to buy it, only..."
Yes...?
"...only, not having read it before, I don't know what the contents are like, do I?"
No, Sir, you have to read them to find out.
"How true! Yes! Still, I expect I'll do so one day."

"I'd like a religious picture..."
Well, we have this one...
"200! Just to hang something over my bed!"
Well, it is by Robert Sargeant Austin...
"Have you anything else, in colour?"
Not in the religious line, I'm afraid.
"Those bulls look nice over there. My daughter keeps cows..."
Mmm.
Goldmark Gallery, Uppingham.

"Mmm, how interesting. By the way, what's today?"
It's Thursday.
"Oh, we go on the steam train today. Goodbye!"
The Book Nook, Fort William.

"Not quite what I was looking for. Someone gave me a large book on golf by Jack Nicklaus. I wanted another, smaller one. You've got a small one but that's by Jack Nicklaus, too, so I think I'll leave it."

"Can I buy all these in one, special, deal?"
Yes... how about £35 the lot?
"Well, it's much more fun buying them when you find them."
If you do, yes.

"Do you sell toilet paper?"
Chapter One Bookshop, Chesham [who refrained from asking 'Hardback or softback, Madam?']

I'LL COOK THEM FOR YOU

"Ooooohhhh! Look at these lovely bindings! I could eat them!"
Once you've paid for them, Madam, I'd be pleased to cook them for you.
The Pudding Bowl, Oundle.

A BOOK IS A BOOK IS A BOOK IS A BOOK IS A BOOK…

Hello, it's Shaun Tyas from Goldmark Books. I'm just ringing to say I'm setting off now, and I'll see you in about half an hour.
"Oh good, I'll move the books out of the shed and into the lounge - should dry them out a bit by the time you're here!"

"Why aren't they all the same thickness? They look so awkward on the shelf!"
Burway Books, Church Stretton.

"Lovely shop! Lots of books! All different colours! Thanks very much. Goodbye."
Goldmark Books, Uppingham.

"Well, I've always said it. If someone can write a book as big as that one, it can only be because they've got something interesting to say!"

"I've got this big bookcase at home. There's about twenty yards of shelving in it. I want to fill it with brown leather. Have you got anything cheap?"
No, you can't get any leather bindings under £6, however useless the contents.
"Mmm."
Tell you what. Why don't you pick a subject, buy one book a week and fill your bookcase over two or three years? You'll have enormous fun doing it and you'll end up with a valuable collection?
"Yeh, but you see it's not the contents I want..."

"Why aren't there any colour illustrations in this? Oh, I know, it's because it's only £20. That one's much better 'cause it's £35!"

"Oh! Old books! I used to have some of them, but I never got on with them!"

"I have a credit for £25."
Yes, that's right.
"Can you show me where the £25-books are, please?"

Comment by the wife of a customer who had sat in his car for over ten minutes trying to read a book on linguistics sold to him by mistake, instead of a book on kite-making, without realising the difference:
"He never was good at reading!"
Bookworm, South Molton.

"Years ago I was hired to catalogue a large library belonging to the High School of a private international school run by nuns here in Rome. After a year and a half of hard work, which included training over thirty students to run the library as a 'vital teaching tool', we invited in the Library Nun who was ostensibly in charge of the whole operation. She looked around at all the tidy shelves and finally said 'Weeeell, it looks quite nice, but don't you think it would be more aesthetically pleasing if you put all the blue books in one place and the red ones in another?'"
Books on Italy, Rome, Italy.

"Are all your gardening books about gardening?"
Goodwin's Booksellers, Leighton Buzzard.

"It is a constant source of amazement to me how many books there are that I don't want to read!"
Goldmark Books, Uppingham.

"The trouble is, it's the French, you see they have to have them in red morocco - yer brown calf just isn't good enough, even if it is contemporary."
A failed attempt to sell a 1st edition Voltaire to a top London shop on the telephone. I got there in the end.

"How much is the chair?"

It's £7,000, Madam.

"Mmm. It's comfortable. We'll have it for the library. Now, books. We'll need four dozen handsome leather bindings."

Yes, we can do that so long as you're willing to pay for them because handsome will be expensive.

"How much are we talking of?"

I should think an average of about £16 each.

"Pah! We'll pay £10. Take it or leave it."

Overheard at an antiques fair and reported by Mike Goldmark.

"Have you any books with bookplates? I collect the bookplates."
Really, how do you get them out?
"Oh, I just cut them out with a razor blade!"
Vivian Wright, Carlisle.

Which of the two would you like, Madam?
"Oh, I think the pink one as they're for girls!"

"Harold used to buy them by the yard! You can't do that anymore, it's such a shame."

"Now, the *ABC of Reading* published by Faber. I'll have it if it's got a street map in it!"
Endcliffe Bookshop, Sheffield.

"It doesn't really matter what's inside, does it?"
Customer admiring fine bindings at Manchester Book Festival, 1989.

VICE

SEX, POLITICS AND RELIGION

Me trying to sell Book-worm Droppings *in Northampton evangelical bookshop:*
Is it a Christian book?
"No, not at all, it's an anthology of amusing remarks overheard in bookshops, and it's very funny!"
Well, you'll have to leave a copy with us, so that we can have a good look at it, to make sure that it's in line with our general ethos.

"Ohh, I *am* tempted!"
Old lady fondling a copy of Dennis Wheatley's The Devil and all his Works *at the bookstall of Mavis Eggle, Harpenden.*

"Are you into all this sort of thing, then?"
Occultique, Northampton.

89

THIS BIZARRE PHENOMENA INDICATES A PHILOSOPHICAL CONUNDRUM ON THE NATURE OF

"Tell me, do you ever get any spirits of the past in here?"
I don't think we…
"I mean, do the previous owners ever come back for their books?"
Goldmark Books, Uppingham.

Elderly German to Jewish dealer, having just completed a deal:
"Have you got any books in German?"
One or two, anything in particular?
"Yes, a song book. We used to sing the songs in the Hitler Youth.
I would like to sing the songs again!"
Goldmark Books, Uppingham.

"Ah ha! I see you've put your copy of *Satanic Verses* upside down!
That's what people used to do with Aleister Crowley titles!"

"Can't stop, but can I use yer toilet? We're 'hunt sabbing' at the
moment and my friend Ian's been arrested!"

"Good morning! I'm the Principal of one of the local Church of
England colleges! Well, our caretaker is retiring soon after thirty
years' service, and so myself and all the staff have had a bit of a
whip-round, and we thought, perhaps get him a *book*! As a leaving
present!"
Yes, certainly. How much did you manage to raise, Canon?
"Five pounds!"
*Later that month the same man was on the Epilogue on television,
talking about the subject of giving and receiving.*
From a bookseller in the North of England.

"'Ere, you can't sell that! Look, it's against the Trades
Discrimination Act!"

"Do you have any husbands upstairs?"
We have a selection upstairs, Madam!
Staniland's, Stamford.

"What's this book about Camp David? He's a friend of mine in
Peterborough!"

"Do you have a section on the OCCULT?"
Yes, here it is...
"Funny the sort of things you can learn about people from their hands..."
Is it? Of course, Sir.
"Even stranger what you can learn about people from their big toes. People wouldn't wear sandals if they knew what I could tell about them!"
Goldmark Books, Uppingham.

"I'd like a Bible, please."
Certainly, which version, Sir?
"There is only one, young man!"
David Johnstone, Eaton Ford.

"Anything on swiving?"
I'm sorry, what does that word mean?
"Pah! Good Anglo-Saxon word, you should know that, young man!"

"I hope you realise I'm a Roman Catholic!"
Sudden revelation of long-term Japanese customer of Andrew Jones, Deddington, Oxford.

"Of course, I know about God. I studied *St. Luke* all last year!"

A nowhere-near-doddery grandmother was shopping among the Ladybirds:
"I want a book that will really tell him what Christmas is all about: you know, with Father Christmas and Christmas trees and tinsel and presents and reindeer and all that!"
Cottage Books, Cullompton.

"Do you have anything on fairies? I've seen some recently!"
Staniland's, Stamford.

"When I was a little girl, I suddenly realised that there wasn't enough time in life to read all the books, so I tended to lose interest. I like to do things properly or not at all. That's why I'm looking forward to going to Heaven, because there's plenty of time there to do all the reading you want!"

Customer spending £5-£6 on Valentine cards:
"It serves me right for having so many girl friends!"
Really? Well, come back next year sir, we're getting braille cards in...
Bibliopol, Northampton.

"Apparently bookshops are romantic places, especially this one, so I've been told. So are art galleries. And flower shops, too."

"You look too normal to be running a shop like this!"
Occultique, Northampton.

"I've been hearing a lot recently about something you chaps call *the physical side* of bookselling. I want to know what it is and how I can get some of it!"

IT JUMPED RIGHT INTO MY HAND

"I have to buy that one. It jumped right off the shelf into my hand!"
Occultique, Northampton.

Two butch teenagers:
"What's this, then?"
"Oh, it's *Death in Venice*. Did you see the film?"
"Yeah, that guy Bogarde played was gay wasn't he?"
"No, just the opposite. He was very sad. He died at the end."
"Oh, yeah..."
David Johnstone, Eaton Ford.

"I'm thinking of moving to Wales and starting to deal in old prints!
So, have you got any old prints of ...a religious nature, or of sheep
perhaps?"
Grafton Country Prints, Oakham.

Hurried, though not yet panicky, woman on the telephone:
"Do you have a copy of *Emergency Childbirth at Home*?"
No...
[*click*]
Los Osos Book Exchange, Los Osos, California.

"Do you sell jock straps?"
Uppingham Bookshop, Uppingham.

"Mmm, yes, *Ribaldry in Ancient Greece*. I think I'll *have* to have
that..."

"You ought to read *The Nature of Atlantis*. It's most interesting. It
was written under THE PRESENCE you know!"
Staniland's, Stamford.

Two men looking at the Bible:
"The man who wrote that must be fair raking it in!"
Hatchard's, Paisley.

"People like you are as dim as a Toc H lamp!"

Seller of dog-eared yoga:
"Would you like to buy these? I don't need them any more because I am God!"
Logos, Sheffield.

"Do you read Greek?"
No, why?
"Well, there's a New Testament downstairs in Greek, and it might tell me about being a born-again Christian. I thought you might read it to me and see."

A woman in a tweed hat (who had already bought some sociology) looked over the shoulder of her prettier Guardian-*carrying companion, who was examining a paperback, and, literally slapping her wrist, said:*
"Put it back! It's written by a man!"
The Saltburn Bookshop, Saltburn.

"You can't use any of the quotes I've given you."
Why? They're harmless enough!
"Because the nature of our work here is unique!"
Evangelical bookstall in Nottingham.

"I'm looking for a wedding gift for a friend. He likes Spanish literature."
Mmm, how about a copy of Cervantes' The Jealous Husband, *Sir?*
"Oh, no, that would be far too near the bone!"
Titles, Oxford.

"I'm looking for two books which I must read. One of them's *Meaning and Truth* by Bertrand Russell, and the other's... well now, I'm not so sure how it's spelled, but THE SPIRIT told me I must get both books. He was most insistent, and I always do everything THE SPIRIT tells me (don't you?). Only, he's not a very good speller!"
An East Midlands public library, probably wanting to remain anonymous in case THE SPIRIT returned!

"Anything on cheeses?"
Try Mowbray's, Sir; we stock very little theology.
An anonymous Cambridge contribution. It has to be the accent,
surely?

DROPPING HOLINESS IN THE BATH

"Have you got *Holiness*? I've dropped mine in the bath!"
Overheard at a Christian Bookshop... makes you think.

"Could you help me with something to amuse my wife?"
The Pudding Bowl, Oundle.

"Have you got the new Tom Jones twelve inch?"
Why? Has he worn out the old one?
David Johnstone, Eaton Ford, when he used to work in a record
shop.

"Have you got *Love*, with perfumed pages?"
Cheyne Lane Bookshop, Stamford.

"I'm looking for a copy of *Lucifer the Great Reformer!*"

"Hello, I'm looking for a copy of *The Joy of Sex.*"
Oh, I'm ever so sorry, but we only have the sequel, More Joy of Sex, *at the moment...*
"Oh, but don't you need Volume One before you go on to Volume Two?"
Mmm, not necessarily... no, I don't think so. Of course, we could get Volume One for you.
"Ah! How long would it take?"
Only two to three days from the wholesaler, I should think.
"Oh, that's no good, we need it in half an hour!"
Hatchard's, Paisley.

A different sort of customer:
"I'm looking for a copy of *The Joy of Sex...*"
Oh, not at the moment I'm afraid, but it wouldn't take us long to get it for you.
"Oh, that's all right, I'm not desperate!"
G.G. Spencer Ltd., Ashford-under-Lyme.

"This shop's gone down a lot. It's far too clean. You could do with some cobwebs in the corners!"
Occultique, Northampton.

"I wonder if you could help me, with some, err, advice?"
Yes, of course, but what's wrong?
"It's my son..."
Oh?
"Yes, I'm so worried about him. I think he might be turning into a... into a... *you know*, one of *those*!"
Ah, but what makes you think that?
"He's started reading ART books!"

99

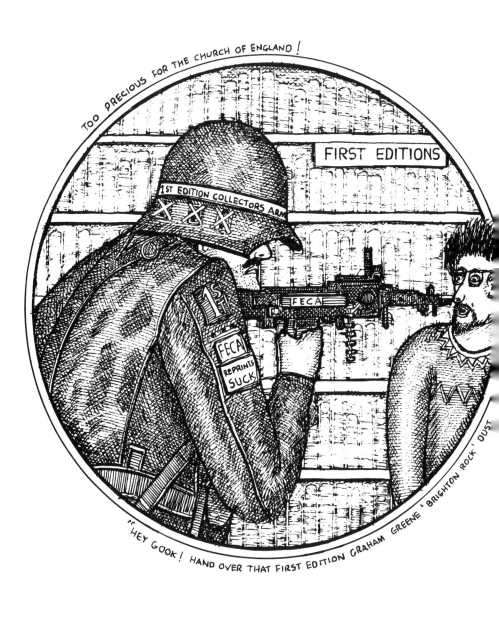

"On the whole I find first edition collectors to be *so* precious that I doubt, *even*, that they would be allowed into the Church of England!"
Staniland's, Stamford.

"Where's the *special* section, dear, you know, *pictures*?"
Post Horn Books, Giggleswick.

"Please describe the smell of each book with your quotation - you never know where these old religious things have been!"
Andrew Stewart, Helpringham.

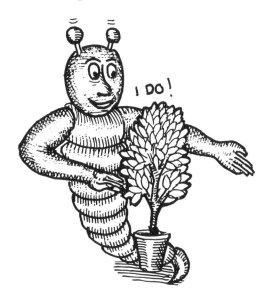

"Look, a word of advice, young lady, while my husband's over there. If you're thinking of getting married, *don't*. Get a green plant instead!"
Godfrey's, York.

"Have you got any non-hagiographical writing?"
Yes Sir! The hagiographical are these two books here, and the non-hagiographical are the rest of the shop!

"Have you got a large print Bible small enough to fit in my handbag?"
A lady with Dr. Who's Tardis disguised as a handbag, at Glance Back Books, Chepstow.

What is it that you were really looking for, Sir?
"A sort of, err, do-it-yourself book on necromancy."
Occultique, Northampton.

Two old ladies picketing Page One, Redcar:
"You can't go in there! They sell *Iron Maiden!*"
This was after they had bought two books on witchcraft for £10 and torn them up on the pavement outside!

"ADVENT CALENDARS - REDUCED!"
Notice in a bookshop window, spotted by Mark English, Bradford, on Christmas Eve.

"I'm looking for a copy of *Sex in Comfort for the Elderly.*"
Old lady, reported by R. Sturgess, Peterborough, overheard in London.

"I promised God that if he got me through my social worker's M.A. degree, I would never open a book again. He did, and I haven't.
Los Osos Book Exchange, Los Osos, California.

103

"Excuse me, but do you have any do-it-yourself books on caning?"
Goldmark Books, Uppingham.

"Can't stop, playing silly buggers tonight!"
Local freemason!

"Have you got a copy of that evangelical book *A Wife in a Sex-Mad Society*?"

"I always go in that bookshop in Bath because it's full of the most wonderful young men! I pretend to look at the books but spend all my time looking at them. They're gorgeous! It makes the books a bit sweaty, though..."

Ah! I see you're buying dinosaur books, Sir!
"Yes, that's right. I like dinosaurs very much."
They are interesting, aren't they?
"Absolutely. You know what I like most about them?"
No?
"They're living proof of the theory of evolution!"

"I'm looking for books on religion..."
Yes, upstairs, Sir, we've got quite a few.
[Customer returns five minutes later]
"No, I just couldn't find any books on snakes!"
Victoria Bookshop, Swindon.

Mmm... NICE!

WELL MAX PROFIT PLC
MEGA £ BOOKS

MILLS & BOON

WE TAKE MORE TO MAKE MORE!

JEFFERY ARCHER HERE

FOR SALE

SMALL BOOKS

SOLD

FOR RE-DEVELOPMENT

BOOK WORM

CLOSING DOWN SALE

BOOK

SOLD

THERE GOES THE NEIGHBOURHOOD ~ THE FUTURE OF THE TRADE?

THE TRADE

Anecdotes which put the trade in a bad light instead!

"Oh hello! It's nice to see you, but I'm sorry I can't look at any of your books at the moment because I've got to go out and get my tobacco crop in!"
A bookseller in the east of England, greeting a rep from The King's England Press.

"The product is padded-out nicely! Weighs about twenty pounds, seems good value!"
A Rep. for Mitchell Beazley, overheard by one of our customers when making an illicit visit to W. H. Smith's.

A friend of mine in a branch of W.H.Smith's, several years ago:
"Hello, do you have a copy of *Private Eye*?
No, we don't at the moment, but we've got True Detective.
"No, it's not that sort of magazine. It's a, err, satirical work."
[*to his wife:*] *Eee, don't he use long words?*

An American at Quinto Bookshop, Cambridge:
"Say! Could you sell me a signed original of the Magna Carta?"
Mmm, not at the moment, I'm afraid, but try across the road:
Deighton Bell might be able to help you!

"It's so difficult compiling a catalogue. The books keep selling before it's issued!"
"Oh, I know, I always keep my best books back now!"
Two dealers overheard at the Northampton Bookfair.

"Can I interest you in any of these? They're mostly trash!"
Well, you'd know all about that, Sir!
[*Excusable rudeness to a customer who writes for* The Sun!]

"Got any books on carrot cakes?"
Try the carrot cake section down the back, next to cephalopodic
brain death.
Blitzgeist Bookshop, Birmingham.

"I'm looking for science fiction. You don't seem to have very much on display. Do you have any reserve stock?"
No, we don't, Sir. You see the problem is, it's SPACE.... And by
that I don't mean outer, I mean out of.
Ernie in a bookshop somewhere in the North.

[A young lady with an extremely greedy and suspicious look brought in ten or so books, "for sale", alias free valuation, all in 'Fraktur-script' German, all oddments, all 'Oxfam material':]
I'm sorry to disappoint you, but these are all odd volumes from incomplete sets, of virtually unknown authors, and even if the sets were complete, they would be quite valueless.
"But look at this, it's surely rare and valuable..." *[her eyes burning in their greed]*
All right, I'll tell you the truth... I cannot afford books of this quality, I doubt if anyone in Birmingham can...
"I don't mind travelling."
...but Blackwells in Oxford might be able to come up with that kind of cash, but whatever you do, don't be hoodwinked.
Blitzgeist Bookshop, Birmingham.

"Got any books on wildfowling?"
Yes, over there, where the gaps in the shelves are!
Goldmark Books, Uppingham.

"Rare books are getting very scarce."
A frustrated dealer at Betty Hyde's, Poole.

"Do you keep stationery here?"
Nah, we occasionally move about.
Blitzgeist Bookshop, Birmingham.

"We've been interviewing people for the gallery job, actually. Interviewed someone yesterday. Super woman! Got on really well with her! Amazing tits she had! I sat there looking at them all the way through the interview. Didn't give her the job, but I nearly said to her 'I'm sorry, I can't give you the job, but could I possibly have a look at your tits because I think they're absolutely phenomenal?' *But I didn't!* Didn't give her the job because, well, what upset me was that she had a boyfriend who was a lorry driver, and I really think we need someone with a bit of class, don't you?"
The proprietor of a famous art gallery!

"Excuse me, but do you have The Wombles?"
No, Madam, I always walk like this.
David Johnstone, Eaton Ford.

"Oh, I do hope they don't bring in VAT on books. The last thing I want to have to do is to start cooking my books four times a year instead of once!"

Customer into exotic leather bindings:
"Hi! Anything to match my green eyes?"
Certainly [slides finger up his nose]
Blitzgeist Bookshop, Birmingham.

FAILED ATTEMPTS TO SELL *BOOK-WORM DROPPINGS* TO THE TRADE
Stories which further illustrate the similarity between the trade and its customers

On the telephone to a bookshop in Grimsby:
"Eee, now then, I don't rightly know. I best go and ask manager. Where was it you said you were ringing from? Port Stanley?"

"I haven't read your *Book-worm Droppings* yet. Of course, I've seen it around the bookshops, but I haven't bought it. I'm waiting to see it in Oxfam."

"A nice book to buy, but I'm not going to!"

"The title is just offensive!"

"You must be joking!"

On the telephone to a bookshop in Wales:
"What sort of a book is it?"
Well, it's a humour book, actually. It's called Book-worm Dropp...
"I don't like humour! I'm buying less and less of it as time goes on..."
Oh, well, I think you'll like this one. It's an anthology of daft remarks overheard in bookshops. A lot of dealers are buying just for their own amusement. It's only £4.95 at retail and I'll give trade terms even on single copies.
"Do you have a distributor?"
No, I'm a small new publisher at the moment, doing everything on my own...
"Well, I can't be bothered to deal with a small new publisher working on his own. People like you are a flaming nuisance. You always want a separate cheque! I use a distributor, it's much simpler. Anyway, we're a very up-market shop so I wouldn't want to stock your nasty little book."
[*And he slammed the telephone down without further comment. What a strange accent English booksellers speak in west Wales.*]

"No, you can't sell anything to *us*. We're a *Christian* bookshop!"

"They're not obscene, are they? Only, it sounds like it to me!"

"Ha! We never deal with anything as *small* as that!"

"No, I didn't like it at all, especially the drawings, I found them far too, err, eschatological... is that the word? Or scatological?"

"We're not bookified here, if you know what I mean!"

"It's for kiddies is it?"
No.
"Mmm, well I don't think it's for us anyway."

"I'd like a copy of *Book-worm Droppings.*"
Oh, thank you very much! Marvellous!
"A hardback."
Really? Oh, that is kind! There are only 500 copies you know!
"But I can't afford it at the moment!"
Ah...
"So, I wondered if you would keep one for me?"
Yes. of course. For how long?
"Well, rather than you actually keep one aside for me, could you tell me when the very last copy is available, and I'll buy it then, before you sell it to anyone else?"

"I'm ever so sorry, but we're just not interested!"
But I haven't told you the title yet!
"I'm still not interested."

Have we dealt with you before?
"No; actually, this is our first title!"
Oh. Well, I think not then. 'Bye. [click]

"No thanks, leave it. It's like incest!"

"We don't deal in one-off publications!"

"We don't buy books from publishers."

PRODUCED BY THE SERIOUS BOOKSHOP LEAGUE (SBL) FOR THEIR CAMPAIGN AGAINST THE PROLIFERATION OF DROPPINGS.

"The owner of the shop is generally only in on Saturday morning."

"Such things are an affront to the management!"

"We've been giggling over it all afternoon, and keep having to read bits out to customers so they don't think we're laughing at them!"

Hello, I've just published this. Can I interest you in stocking it?
"Absurd remarks? We don't get any of those here."
Oh, well, I'll leave you looking at it, while I look round, if I may...?
[Later I returned to the desk and asked the young man in a suit:]
Well, what do you think? Would you like some for stock, perhaps on a sale-or-return basis? I've given a review copy to your local paper, too.
"I can't sell that. Not here."
Oh dear! Well, never mind. I'm going to produce a second volume, perhaps you have some anecdotes you'd like to share with me?
"Look, my customers are sensible, sensitive and articulate people! Frankly, I find your suggestion gratuitously offensive. Kindly leave the shop."
[It was in a town on the north-east coast!]

A Canadian tourist bought a pile of local topography in our shop, so I drew his attention to Book-worms, *on the grounds that it counted as a local item:*
"Oh! That's nice. How much is it?"
Only £4.95...
"Mmm. Well, I'll be returning to England in four years' time. I might be able to afford it then. You'll still have some, won't you?"

At the post office:
"That's too heavy! The Australians are not keen on junk mail!"

"No, we're a new bookshop, not second-hand."
But this is a new book!
"I'm still not interested."

"No, but we don't stock new books. We're a second-hand bookshop."

"There's no point, we're closing down next week!"

OTHER COMMENTS ON
BOOK-WORM DROPPINGS

"...it's nice to know that other booksellers suffer!"

"Look, Shaun, just stop it now, this writing down everything I say. It's got more than a bit irritating."

"Reading it was...a deeply moving experience!"
Hatchard's of Paisley.

"Please forgive delay in payment - couldn't stop laughing long enough to write the cheque!"

"Please find enclosed cheque to cover invoice 829 for five copies of that *yellow* book, still can't remember what it's called, but it had *pages* with lots of writing and pictures on them!"

Hello! It's Paul Watkins Publishing, here. You very kindly ordered two copies of Book-worm Droppings...
"Yes..."
I'm just ringing to check whether you wanted the hardback or the paperback?
"Ah, hang on a moment, I'll just put you through to natural history...!"
[*It was a leading London shop!*]

"I've read your *Book-worm Droppings* and I'm very worried about you!"
Really? Why?
"Well, it's only natural to be worried about someone who has bizarre things said to him all day long. It isn't normal. I think you attract them. You're a sort of loony fly paper."

A Letter from America:
"I have just about split my sides while reading over breakfast Wayne Somers' review in *The Book Source Monthly* of *Book-worm Droppings.* Somehow it is comforting to know that we do not on this side of the Great Water have a monopoly on crass insensitivity."

"My library is Dewey-Decimalized. How dare you write a book with no Dewey-Decimal Classification whatsoever!"

"I read your book. Nice little book. Nice job. Don't think I'll be buying a copy. But I particularly liked the quotation from the man who said that he had a book, in his house, and that it helped him to get to sleep at night. I agreed with that, because I keep a book by my bed, but I usually manage only a few pages rather than a few paragraphs like your man. Still, I agreed with the sentiment. It is a good idea to have a book in the house, isn't it?"

I related the above incident in the pub and got the following response:
"Well, that's true! I keep a book by my bed, too. But I only manage a few lines before I nod off. I've been trying to read the same book now for two or three years..."

"It should have been printed on a high-acid paper so that it rotted away as soon as possible!"

"Shaun, for goodness sake print the next volume on absorbent paper. It would be so much more convenient."
Mike Goldmark.

115

THEY SEEMED AWFUL DIRTY, SO I WASHE...

An old lady had invited a dealer to come to her house to see some books she wanted to sell. The titles were very exciting so the dealer drove there at high speed in great excitement:

Dealer: Err, what are those things lying on your settee?

Old Lady: "They're the books! I looked at them and they seemed awful dirty, so I washed them..."

Reported by Jane Hilton, Bakewell.

A SECTION OF UTTER MADNESS
TO FINISH OFF!

KEEP IT UNDER YOUR HAT!

QUESTION YOUR REALITY

WAH HOO!

YOU MUST BE MAD TO HAVE GOT THIS FAR, READING ALL THOSE ENDLESSLY INANE QUOTES! NOW YOU ARE ABOUT TO GO OVER THE EDGE — INTO THE BLOATED BOWELS OF THE BOOKWORM!

Hello! How are you?
"Oh, very well thank you. I've just bought an axe."
Oh yes? And, err, what are you going to use it for?
"For chopping down trees. People keep wanting to conserve them, but in my opinion there's far too many trees in the world. They're always getting in the way! I think that they should all be chopped down after they've reached 18". I'm quite in favour of planting trees, but if we chopped more of them down, we'd be able to plant more, wouldn't we? Anyway, enough of that, have you got any books on mind control?"

"Are we alone? I must tell you. I never read books written by women writers. It's not that I've got anything against women. Quite the contrary! It's just that it simplifies things so much when browsing through bookshops. As for Virago Classics, well! The name puts me off for a start. I wouldn't want to have anything to do with a Virago, if you get my meaning. However, Marie Bashkirtseff seems a fascinating travel writer... Dervla Murphy, Cycling to India, that sort of thing. Can't stand her as a writer. I've read everything she's written, so I ought to know!"

Two ladies in the street:
"Well I'm ever so worried about my husband."
"Oh dear, why's that? Is he ill?"
"I think he is, but when I went to the doctor he didn't seem that interested. Said there was nothing that could be done unless he was willing to volunteer for treatment, as he wasn't dangerous like. I suppose I shall just have to put up with it now."
"Oh, that sounds terrible! I am sorry. But, what sort of things has he been doing?"
"Well, oh it's sad, he's always been such a good husband, but, lately, he's been going off to the library, and he comes home with these books, and, do you know, sometimes he sits there reading them for as long as an hour at a time!"
The second lady was a customer of a shop which wanted to remain anonymous.

"Hello, it's nice to see you again. You know, I was only thinking the other day, about some time back. My wife and I..., don't get me wrong, we're very happily married, we are. Yes, very well suited. Anyway, I was lying in bed thinking 'You know, it doesn't really mean all that much, if all I've got left to look forward to is another twenty years or so of marriage, *like this*', and life just didn't seem worth living, but then, I thought to myself 'get a book!'. So I did. I reached out and picked one from the bookcase (I keep a few books by the bed) and, do you know, it made all the difference! And ever since then, I've always wanted to be a writer!"

"I'm a spiritual sort of person, so I *understand* things, and I *feel* things, deeply, and I can tell that there's a book in this shop for me! I had the same feeling when I was in Glastonbury last. We were driving along and I said 'Stop the car! There's a book in that shop for me!' So, we stopped and went in, and (sure enough!), there it was: I found it in ten seconds, and, do you know, I'm getting the same feeling...? Oh! Ahhh! Hang on a minute, it's different... Ah, yes, I can tell, you did have a book I wanted but you sold it two weeks ago. In fact I can tell you that it was a book I really needed, and you sold it within the last ten days...!"

GET OUT! GET OUT! GET OUT!

ANOTHER SOCRATIC DIALOGUE, THIS TIME RECORDED AT A PRIVATE MEETING OF THE STAMFORD BRANCH OF BOOKAHOLICS ANONYMOUS, SELF-HELP CO-COUNSELLING GROUP.

Well, I think perhaps one of us had better open up a little. Perhaps say a few words about himself, why he's come to the group and what he hopes to get out of it. Shaun, perhaps you could help the rest of us? At your own pace now...

Thank you, Bob. Yes. Err. Where do I start? I was fifteen years old when I began to realise that I had, err, a *problem*, with, err, with *books*. I used to go down to the local Toc H every Saturday morning and come back with lots of them. The lady there let me and my brother take away as much as we could carry for half a crown. I soon built up quite a collection of Victorian books on women missionaries and out-of-date maths textbooks. I regret it now, but it seemed fun at the time. You see, it wasn't long before I began to move on to the, to the, to the *harder* stuff.

Oh no! Dear, dear.

Yes, I began to collect books on the Anglo-Saxons and the Vikings.

Then I went to University and I met others, like me, and we formed a group of, well, *friends*, and we'd meet every week and fondle the bindings in our collections, and drink cups of tea, and it was quite nice really. But afterwards...the loneliness really hurt.

Oh, we all know about that, Shaun! Go on, you're with friends now!

It was an illusion. Owning the books didn't mean possessing the knowledge within them. How I deceived myself!

Too true! Too true!

When I left University I joined the second-hand book trade. It was the only way I could continue to feed my vice in the quantities I now needed. There was no stopping me. I bought and bought and bought. Soon I'd collected so many volumes of the, err, *hard stuff*, that I had to broaden my field, just so I could keep going: I started collecting historical novels about the Anglo-Saxons as well! I'm *sorry*. It wasn't long before I became the bookshop's single best customer! On *my* wages! Most of the time I paid for the books straight away, but, then, err, I started running an *account*, and before long I owed the shop £1675! Then, the trouble really started. *Look, it's all right if you don't want to go on...*

It's o.k. No, really, it's all right. I can make it. I just feel so *embarrassed*. You see, the books had been breeding, and there was no space left at home. A quarter of the house was used as storage, and all the books were in boxes. I couldn't even look at them any more! I spent two years trying to catalogue them but only got half way. I discovered I'd accumulated about seven thousand volumes. At first, you know, I was happy with *reading copies*. Then I started getting off on variant editions, first editions, copies with different bindings. Proof copies. All of the same titles! There was no sense in it. It was hopeless. And I spent all my time thinking about the ones I hadn't got rather than the ones I had. I was doing about fifty books a week then, and never reading anything.

Then I did start reading, but it was *bibliographies*. And I started making lists of the books I still wanted. Can you imagine it? Just sitting there day after day reading books about books? And I kept muttering to myself 'floor to ceiling, wall-to-wall shelving - it beats decorating any day!'
This is too much. You've really been through it, haven't you?

You haven't heard of the *last stage* yet. I was so hung up on my, err, *problem*, that I compiled a book celebrating it, and I called it, *Book-worm Droppings*. Would you believe it? Then I realised that publishing books was just the *terminal* stage.

I'd got so obsessed with thinking about the ones I hadn't got, the ones I thought I really needed, that I went into publishing on my own, so I could publish the missing titles. The first one was *Anglo-Saxon Writs*. And you know what self-employment means, don't you? Keeping books! It all seems so senseless now. More titles followed. I was hooked. If it wasn't for this group, I wouldn't know where to turn. IT WAS TOC H WHAT DONE IT, YOU KNOW! That's the wrong turn I made!

Well, it's very good that you've identified the problem and are taking positive steps to do something about it. Anyway, enough of that! Isn't it nice to have a book in the house? When's the next meeting? I'll bring my Camden's Britannica - the one with the fine 17th-century calf, raised bands and dentelled tooling. Ooohhh it's exciting!

ANSWERS TO QUIZ TIME

1. Roget's *Thesaurus of English Words and Phrases*. Peter Mark Roget first published the work in 1852.

2. Roget's *Thesaurus of English Words and Phrases*.

3. Roget's *Thesaurus of English Words and Phrases*.

4. Roget's *Thesaurus of English Words and Phrases*.

5. *Tess of the D'Urbervilles*, first published in 1891, the famous novel by Thomas Hardy (1840-1928).

6. Vita Sackville West (1892-1962)! It might be significant that she was the author of *All Passion Spent* (1931), but it probably isn't.

7. Ephemera. It means items of temporary use, like posters and bus tickets. Some people collect them.

8. Possibly *The Pink Fairy Book*, by Andrew Lang (1844-1912), but could be any!

9. Oscar Wilde, Irish poet, wit and dramatist (1854-1900).

10. *The Rubá'iyát of Omar Khayyám*. First translated by Edward Fitzgerald, published in 1859, but the original is in 12th century Persian.

11. Stephen Hawking's *Brief History of Time* (1988).

12. *Ibid* is an abbreviation of the Latin *ibidem* meaning 'in the same place' (e.g., book or chapter), often also used to mean 'by the same person'. It is also an abbreviation for International Bibliographical Description.

13. Robert J. Foster, *The Complete Guide to Middle Earth* (1978), a guide to Tolkien's *Lord of the Rings*.

14. For missile read Missal! A Missal is a book containing the service of the Mass for the whole year.

15. *Ulysses*, the novel by James Joyce (1882-1941), was first published in 1922.

16. *The Book of Changes* is also called the *I Ching*. It is at least 5000 years old and is the central text of ancient Chinese philosophy.

17. *Love in the Time of Cholera* (1984) by the Colombian novelist Gabriel García Márquez (b.1928).

18. Samuel Pepys (1633-1703) wrote his own diary, from 1660 to 1669. It was first published in 1825 but the first full edition is that

edited by R. Latham and W. Matthews in 11 volumes published between 1970 and 1983. His name is pronounced 'Peeps' (usually).

19. Thomas Hardy's *Jude the Obscure* was first published in 1895, by Macmillan.

20. Salman Rushdie's *The Satanic Verses* (1988).

21. Patrick Leigh Fermor (b.1915).

22. Joseph Heller (b.1923) wrote *Catch 22*, published in 1961.

23. The customer actually wanted a book on *Genealogy for Beginners*, probably the one by A. J. Willis (1984). Genealogy is tracing family trees, but family trees are caused by gynaecology.

24. *The Expectant Mariner*, by Shirley Deane, published in 1962.

25. Kaffe Fasset is the author of the knitting book intended.

26. *Family: Ties that Bind and Gag* by Erma Bombeck; the Pan edition appeared in 1988.

27. The customer wanted a book on bloodstock breeding, perhaps Sir Charles Leicester's *Bloodstock Breeding*, ed. H. Wright (1983).

28. Another warped reference to *The Rubá'iyát of Omar Khayyám*.

29. Unidentifiable: if you know it please send information to Paul Watkins Publishing for correction in next edition.

30. The man actually wanted a laundrette.

31. There are many. Sorry, unidentifiable.

32. Arthur Mee (1875-1943) published the King's England series between 1936 and 1953. A modern facsimile reprint is under production by the King's England Press, Barnsley.

33. Theodore Sturgeon's *Not without Sorcery*.

34. Actually Penguin Books no. 1152, which happens to be H. E. Bates' *The Purple Plain*.

35. Sorry, unidentifiable.

36.John Ernest Steinbeck (1902-1968), American author of the novel *To a God Unknown* (1933).

37. Sir Arthur Conan Doyle (1859-1930). He wrote the Sherlock Holmes series, published between 1887 and 1902.

38. Euripides, the ancient Greek playwright, lived between 480 and 406 B.C. 18 of his plays survive, including the *Bacchae*.

39. Sean O'Casey (1884-1964), Irish playwright.

40. George Bernard Shaw (1856-1950), Irish playwright and man of letters, wrote the play *Captain Brassbound's Conversion*.

41. *Howards End*, by E. M. Forster (1879-1970), published in 1910.

42. Unidentifiable.

43. Kingsley Amis (b.1922), English novelist.

44. Unfortunately, it wasn't H. G. Wells (1866-1946), who published *The Outline of History* in 1920. He is the most obvious candidate, but the customer wanted something else. So, unidentifiable.

45. C. S. Lewis (1898-1963) published *The Lion, the Witch and the Wardrobe* in 1950.

46. *The Book of Revelation* or *The Revelation of St John the Divine*, last book of the New Testament.

47. H. E. Bates (1905-74), British novelist, playwright and short story writer, of course!

48. Judith (or Judy) Garland (1922-1969) and Dirk Bogarde (1921-) made the film in 1963.

49. Miguel de Cervantes Saavedra (1547-1616) wrote *Don Quixote de la Mancha*. Or was it the Muncher? Anyway, it was published between 1604 and 1615 and has been a best-seller ever since.

50. The customer meant the Apocrypha, a selection of books which are of great historical interest but not recognised by all believers to be part of the 'inspired' Bible. The name means 'hidden things', appropriately enough. An apothecary is a chemist.

51. Evelyn Waugh (1903-1966), English novelist, whose name is pronounced 'Waw, was a man.

52. Johann Wolfgang von Goethe (1749-1832), whose name is pronounced 'Gurta'.

53. Mahogany wardrobes.

54. Iris Murdoch (b.1919), novelist, is actually Irish.

55. Ferdinand Magellan (1480-1521), Portuguese navigator.

56. John le Carré (b.1931), British novelist, not Robert le Carrier, chef.

57. Not *Nostromo* (1904) by Joseph Conrad (1857-1924), but the French astrologer Nostradamus (or Michel de Notredame) (1503-1566). His *Centuries of Predictions* appeared in 1555-58.

58. Kate Greenaway (1846-1901), English illustrator, not Shakespeare's wife Anne Hathaway.

59. Mummy was thinking of Edward Lear (1812-88), the famous writer of limericks. Oscar Wilde is item no. 9.

60. Angus Wilson (b.1913), English novelist and author of *The Old Men at the Zoo* (1961), in which a man is kicked by a giraffe!

61. Librarian sixth sense identified *The Leopard Hunts in Darkness*, published in 1984 by Wilbur Smith (b.1933), English novelist.

62. Ebenezer Cobham Brewer (1810-1897) wrote the celebrated *Dictionary of Phrase and Fable*, first published in 1870, which is not about brewing but about literature.

63. *Love in a Cold Climate*, the novel by Nancy Mitford, published in 1984. Some confusion with no. 17 clearly in operation.

64. No, Marc Chagall was a Russian artist, born in 1889.

65. Not Enid Blyton but *The Kama Sutra*(!), the classic early Indian text on erotica, attributed to Vátsyáyana in the 7th century AD. The classic English translation is that by Richard Burton, first published discreetly in 1883.

66. The poor customer was in search of a *note book*.

67. *The Demon Lord of Karanda* by David Eddings, published in 1988.

68. Collins have published some marvellous field guides, but not that one.....yet.

69. *J. M. Barrie and the Lost Boys*, by Andrew Birkin (1986).

70. Possibly *Schindler's Ark*, by Thomas Kenealy (published in 1982), but perhaps more likely to be *Kruger's Alp*, a book about a mountain, by Christopher Hope (1984).

71. John Steinbeck again, this time as the author of the famous *The Grapes of Wrath*, published in 1939. Of course! If you thought of *The Wild Bunch*, by Don Shiach (1990), you did well!

72. She *must* have meant a book on rearing peacocks. Possibly thinking of the word *Harnessing*? Sometimes all you can do is repeat the initial response.

73. For *Lice* read *Life*.

74. Unidentifiable, but I think it was a serialisation, perhaps as a magazine, of true crime. Write to us if you know it.

75. *Young Men in Spats*, by P. G. Wodehouse (1881-1975), published in 1957.

76. *The Man who mistook his Wife for a Hat*, by Oliver W. Sacks (1985). The real title is just as bizarre.

77. Yes, they are!

SCORES: If you scored **less than 25** you are suffering from book-starvation and should visit your local bookseller and library more often. **25-40** you're not doing badly, but could do better. **40-60** you are a well-informed, well-balanced individual who keeps his booking under control and knows how to use a book and when and where to do so. **Over 60**, I'm sorry but you are in serious danger of becoming a bibliomaniac, if not a bookaholic. Perhaps you are one already. I recommend that you join your local Bookaholics Anonymous immediately, or form your own support group!

See you in Volume Three!

Shaun, Martin and what's his name?
Oh yes! Watkins of Stamford.